W9-BYM-252

Praise for
Forty Loaves

"Christians with questions? It used to be, in certain circles, that even raising a question disqualified the questioner from the discussion. Any question was taken as a sign of doubt, which called in question the steadiness of one's faith. Yet secretly, most believers struggle with nagging queries about life and God. C. David Baker, in this open-minded yet faithful book, speaks to doubters who long to believe, and addresses some of life's troubling issues from the inside out. A great encouragement for doubters and trusters both."

—LUCI SHAW, author of *The Crime of Living Cautiously* and
Breath for the Bones; Writer in Residence, Regent College,
Vancouver, British Columbia

"C. D. Baker has given a gift to every honest Christian, to wit, profound insight and amazing affirmation about questions honest Christians ask…but sometimes were afraid to express to others. This book looks at the "elephant in the room" and kisses that elephant on the lips with such gracious, loving biblical wisdom that you will rise up and call Baker blessed. And you will rise up and call me blessed for recommending it to you."

—STEVE BROWN, professor at Reformed Theological
Seminary in Orlando, author, and president of the media
ministry of Key Life Network, Inc.

"In contrast to the easy, trite, and ultimately unsatisfying 'good news' that is peddled in pop Christianity, *Forty Loaves* provides the space to explore what Christians often feel but are afraid to express. Baker's timely reflections on the complexities of faith in today's world will help to nurture integrity within people of faith in a way that can only result in an enhanced relationship with God and with others."

—BRUCE W. LONGENECKER, W. W. Melton Chair
of Religion, Baylor University

"Fresh-baked wisdom for all who've dined on the stale, hardened dinner rolls of sin. C. D. Baker serves up a bread that satisfies!"

—RAY BLACKSTON, author of *Flabbergasted*

40 loaves

40 loaves

Breaking Bread with Our
Father Each Day

c. d. baker
author of *101 Cups of Water*

WATERBROOK
PRESS

FORTY LOAVES
PUBLISHED BY WATERBROOK PRESS
12265 Oracle Boulevard, Suite 200
Colorado Springs, Colorado 80921

All Scripture quotations, unless otherwise indicated, are taken from the New American Standard Bible®.
© Copyright The Lockman Foundation 1960, 1962, 1963, 1968, 1971, 1972, 1973, 1975, 1977, 1995.
Used by permission. (www.Lockman.org). Scripture quotations marked (NIV) are taken from the Holy
Bible, New International Version®. NIV®. Copyright © 1973, 1978, 1984 by International Bible Society.
Used by permission of Zondervan Publishing House. All rights reserved. Scripture quotations marked
(NLT) are taken from the Holy Bible, New Living Translation, copyright © 1996. Used by permission of
Tyndale House Publishers Inc., Wheaton, Illinois 60189. All rights reserved. Scripture quotations marked
(KJV) are taken from the King James Version.

Italics in Scripture quotations reflect the author's added emphasis.

Prayers ending chapters 3, 5, 7, 8, 10, and 13 were translated from the original German sources by Catherine Winkworth (1827–1878). Prayers without attributions are the work of the author.

ISBN 978-0-307-44490-5
ISBN 978-0-307-44491-2 (electronic)

Published in association with the literary agency of Alive Communications Inc., 7680 Goddard Street,
Suite 200, Colorado Springs, CO 80920, www.alivecommunications.com.

Published in the United States by WaterBrook Multnomah, an imprint of the Crown Publishing Group,
a division of Random House Inc., New York.

WATERBROOK and its deer colophon are registered trademarks of Random House Inc.

Library of Congress Cataloging-in-Publication Data
Baker, C. D. (Charles David), 1951–
   40 loaves : breaking bread with our Father each day / by C.D. Baker.—1st ed.
       p. cm.
   ISBN 978-0-307-44490-5—ISBN 978-0-307-44491-2 (electronic)
1. Disappointment—Religious aspects—Christianity. 2. Consolation—Prayers and devotions. I. Title.
II. Title: Forty loaves.
   BV4905.3.B35 2009
   248.8'6—dc22

                                        2009017142

Printed in the United States of America
2009—First Edition

10 9 8 7 6 5 4 3 2 1

SPECIAL SALES
Most WaterBrook Multnomah books are available at special quantity discounts when purchased in bulk
by corporations, organizations, and special-interest groups. Custom imprinting or excerpting can also be
done to fit special needs. For information, please e-mail SpecialMarkets@WaterBrookMultnomah.com
or call 1-800-603-7051.

Contents

Contents

Wisdom is found
when troubled hearts
ask honest questions.

Dear Reader,

Do you ask yourself many questions? I don't mean questions like, "Why can't I resist chocolate ice cream?" I mean probing, sometimes embarrassing questions about how you relate to your faith. Questions like, "Why does God seem silent?" or "Why don't I have much faith?"

Unfortunately, most of us are reluctant to admit we have questions like these. Many of our church communities have led us to believe that certainty and confidence are proof of true spirituality. Bewilderment or—worse yet, doubt—is seen as a sign of weakness.

Besides, questions disturb things.

Maybe questions embarrass some people or threaten them; maybe they seem rebellious, even sinful. Whatever the reasons, many of us feel the need to keep our questions to ourselves. Ironically, we even try keeping them from God.

What a shame.

A German linguist once made the odd observation that the punctuation marks of our lives say something about us. And he was convinced that the question mark was the most meaningful mark of all.

Questions invite authenticity. Questions give us permission to wonder. Questions open the door for wisdom. Asking opens our eyes to ourselves. Asking opens our hearts to the Spirit.

Indeed, someone has said that it's always a more beautiful answer to ask a more beautiful question.

However, I should warn you, questions *do* disturb things. Seeing ourselves more clearly is not always comfortable—but it is always good. Increased self-awareness can refresh our relationships with God and others…and can lead to healthy self-acceptance.

40 Loaves is inspired by Christian strugglers—people wandering through the wilderness of their own souls, not always fitting in, yet asking from and sharing with others those precious bits of bread they find while struggling along the way. It is my hope that, like them, you and I will be nourished with the wisdom that comes from asking and sharing the right questions.

"Jesus said to them, 'I am the bread of life; he who comes to Me will not hunger, and he who believes in Me will never thirst'" (John 6:35).

Grace and peace be with you always,

C. D. Baker

Why do I want
Jesus in my life?

I KNOW A WOMAN WHO SPENT years doing all the things the preacher said a good follower of Jesus should do: she obeyed the preacher's rules, she worked hard at believing, she prayed faithfully, and she mailed her checks regularly to the address on the television screen.

But one evening she wrestled with an uncomfortable realization. She found herself staring at a picture of Jesus, only to feel resentment instead of love. It was then that she had to admit to herself that the Jesus she knew exhausted her.

She turned away from the picture, suddenly realizing that she had not wanted Jesus in her life out of love for him. He was too hard to love. Yet she still wanted Jesus in her life. Why?

Then it hit her like a bucket of cold water.

She had wanted Jesus in her life for her sake alone. She wanted material blessings. She wanted to feel righteous and maybe superior to others. She wanted peace and joy. And she wanted Jesus close so he wouldn't punish her—something of a fire insurance policy to keep her out of hell.

But she didn't really want Jesus.

I wonder why I really want Jesus in my life. Do I really want to take him *by* the hand or just take *from* his hand?

Like the woman above, could it be that the Jesus I know is some cosmic force I fearfully try to manipulate for my benefit? Is that why I focus on his gifts and dodge his anger, all the while avoiding his eyes?

I'm afraid I do sometimes feel this way and, frankly, it's no wonder many of us do.

Many of us have only ever been shown Performance Jesus—a "carrot and stick" Jesus. On the one hand, this Performance Jesus doles out blessings if we toe the line, and on the other, he's ready to strike us hard for disobeying. He's a daunting presence that we need to either appease or avoid.

Most of us know people like that…

We call them abusers.

Do we really want them in our lives? Of course not. In fact, we shouldn't. So why would we want *that* Jesus in our lives? We shouldn't.

Unfortunately, performance Christianity unwittingly presents just that kind of Jesus. Performance Christianity keeps many from seeing Gospel Jesus, and so we don't experience Jesus's love. Without feeling his love, it's hard—actually it's impossible—to love him. So we obey him out of self-interest and fear but never follow him out of love and gratitude.

But there is good news.

The Jesus of the gospel very much wants us to want him in our lives. He understands why we've struggled to love him. He feels our anger with that other Jesus, but he wants to reintroduce himself as he really is.

Gospel Jesus is the only person in the universe who truly loves us as we are.

And he has a gift waiting to pour into our opened hearts. It's called grace.

So let's ask him for the gift…every day. Let's ask him to show us how much he loves us in spite of ourselves. Let's ask him to teach us the gospel daily—to remind us over and over that he loves his children no matter what.

Let's ask him daily to show himself as he really is—a big lover of big sinners.

And when he answers us, we will be changed. No longer will we obey for our own gain, but instead we will simply follow him, and gladly. For each time we feel his love overflowing in our hearts, spilling over into every part of our being and bursting beyond ourselves in love for others, we will love him again, and again, and again (see 1 John 4:19).

Those are the times we will really want Jesus in our lives.

Those are the only times we *can* really want Jesus in our lives.

Food for Thought

When have I used Jesus for my own purposes?
What are the things I expect Jesus to do for me?
Can I honestly say that I *love* Jesus?
How would I describe Jesus to someone else?
Do I really understand how much Jesus loves me…no
matter what?

A PRAYER

O Lord, how dry I am without Jesus.
How foolish and vain
When I desire anything but him.
For what, without Jesus, can the world
give me?
Let me love all things for the sake of Jesus
But let me love Jesus for his own sake.

ADAPTED FROM *THE IMITATION OF CHRIST*,
THOMAS À KEMPIS (1380–1471)

Why am I so uncomfortable with doubts?

A young woman I know recently remarked that her life is made miserable by doubts. She said that her unhappiness started when she began to doubt a few points of her church's doctrines. She began to panic. She thought if she doubted a few things, she would soon doubt everything, and that would leave her in a place of disbelief.

I told her I doubted that would happen. She didn't appreciate that.

Another friend doubted her salvation to the point of depression. Her church insisted that "knowing" was to be the source of her assurance.

I invited her to doubt her church. She was too afraid.

I wonder: are doubts the bane of faith or faith's driving edge?

In the examples above, healthy doubts and hard questions could have been doorways for many to know God more deeply. Instead, a desperate need for certainty prevented authentic encounters with God.

Doubts threaten our sense of control, don't they?

As church communities and as individuals we prefer to be sure about things, but doubts have a way of disrupting our confidence—our control. They lead to worry, fear, and insecurity. But here's an idea to consider:

What if our discomfort with doubt is really a symptom of an addiction to control?

Doubts also threaten our foundations. We think we must be absolutely certain about the things we believe. Otherwise, how could we survive? We've come to trust our *knowing*. So, what about this:

What if our discomfort with doubt is a symptom of misplaced faith?

Maybe we should look at doubting a different way. After all, who said doubting must always be a bad thing? Jesus instructed Thomas to "stop doubting and believe" (John 20:27, NIV). Does that mean that all doubt is bad? What if doubt and faith are sometimes related?

Martin Luther observed that the opposite of faith is not doubt or unbelief but rather self-reliance. Healthy doubt can actually drive us to faith by putting us beyond ourselves.

Most of us see doubting Thomas in an unfair light. Few of us want to be like him, do we? But, if we're honest, most of us *are* like him. We do secretly wonder about the things we say we believe. That's reality.

At least Thomas had the courage to admit his doubts.

Did that make him a bad disciple? What did Jesus do when he learned of Thomas's doubts?

Did he rebuke him? No.

Did he shame him? No.

Jesus invited Thomas to explore his doubts…to come close to him and touch him *so that he might believe.*

Healthy, humble doubt simply wants to know Truth (Jesus) better.

So, what if we gave ourselves permission to doubt, at least once, the spiritual ideas we've been taught to believe? Now, I'm not talking about closed-minded cynicism like Zacharias's dismissal of the angel's promise (see Luke 1:18). That earned him a pretty stiff rebuke.

I am talking about sincere, yearning doubt like Mary revealed to the angel who foretold her virgin birth (see Luke 1:34). This is not scoffing dismissal; this is the kind of humble doubt *that longs to believe.* This is the kind of doubt we find in Matthew 28 when some of Jesus's disciples came to worship the risen Lord…*while still doubting.*

Humble doubt offered in a spirit of honest suspicion invites the Holy Spirit to teach and to inspire deeper and deeper faith within us. It liberates us to cry, "I do believe; help my unbelief" (Mark 9:24).

Food for Thought

When do I wrestle with doubts? Do I feel guilty when I do?

What do I think of others who have doubts?

Is it okay to not always be sure?

Is my faith more in my certainties or more in a Jesus of some mystery?

A PRAYER

While Faith is with me, I am blest;
It turns my darkest night to day;
But while I clasp it to my breast,
I often feel it slide away....
Oh, help me, God! For thou alone
Canst my distracted soul relieve;
Forsake it not: it is thine own,
Though weak, yet longing to believe.

ANNE BRONTË (1820–1849),
FROM "THE DOUBTER'S PRAYER"

3

Why can't I overcome
sin in my life?

I heard a popular radio preacher say that he had not sinned for three days. I turned to my wife. "Gee. What's the matter with me? I can't go sinless for three seconds."

"Three seconds? You're being easy on yourself."

I wasn't amused. I actually felt guilty. "I guess I need to try harder."

Guilt?

Try harder?

These are common responses from those of us who limit sin to willful bad behavior—naughty deeds that can be overcome with a little more spiritual horsepower.

But Jesus teaches us what sin *really* looks like by reminding us of sin's opposite: obedience. Obedience is loving God with *all* our hearts, souls, and minds, and loving our neighbors as ourselves (see Matthew 22:37–40).

Anything less is sin.

Gulp.

This means I'm sinning whenever I fail to love God and others *with everything I am.* And Jesus isn't talking about just doing the "best I can do." He's talking about PERFECTION (see Matthew 5). So with perfection as the standard, how do any of us overcome sin in our lives?

We don't.

So how did the preacher go sinless for three days?

He didn't.

"If we say that we have no sin, we are deceiving ourselves and the truth is not in us" (1 John 1:8).

The sad truth is that until the resurrection, we *are* sinners—like the gallery of the faithful in Hebrews 11. That's a gallery of forgiven sinners like us who demonstrated halfheartedness, deceit, disobedience, and pride...as well as faithfulness and righteousness. Think about it:

Noah did the whole naked drunk thing.

Abraham lied about his wife to save his own neck.

Sarah mocked God's promise.

Moses had an anger problem.

We all know about David.

And we don't want to forget about good Peter's denials of Christ in the gospels. I could go on.

So where does this leave us? As struggling sinners in need of constant forgiveness.

But how do we finally overcome sin in our lives? *We* don't.

But some of us keep trying to come up with a plan anyway. In my case, I'm always tempted to redefine sin as something more manageable, like a list of external behaviors that I *can* do...maybe even for three days. But that eventually messes things up, because an inaccurate understanding of sin leads to inaccurate ideas about the Christian life.

So when that doesn't work out, I begin excusing myself as "only human." But though that may be true, it's really no excuse.

Actually, none of our strategies work—not when God demands perfection.

But there is good news.

Sin has already been overcome *for* us *by* Christ.

"For *sin shall not be master over you,* for you are not under law but under grace" (Romans 6:14).

Does this mean we are able to NOT ever sin? No.

But it does mean that Christ has rendered our sins powerless to *condemn us.*

Believing that can change the way we live. J. B. Phillips wrote, "I am quite certain that [God] does not want us to waste any time raking over our sins. He wants us to accept His forgiveness and walk forward confidently in His strength."

Okay, fine. But if we're not sinless, can't we at least sin *less*?

Yes. The power to sin less comes from receiving the gospel—the unconditional forgiveness of Christ—over and over again.

Confessing sin is liberating; receiving grace is empowering.

Confession puts the gospel to work. Yet, just like the early church, we seem to forget the good news. Paul wrote, "Do you think lightly of the riches of His kindness and tolerance and patience, not knowing that *the kindness of God leads you to repentance*?" (Romans 2:4).

Asking ourselves why we can't overcome sin is a wonderful question; it means we care.

But asking the Spirit about our sin is better.

Gospel-gratitude mysteriously enables us to cooperate with the Spirit in taking a few more small steps toward the final hope of our perfection-yet-to-come.

Food for Thought

Does sin bother me?

How have I defined *sin*?

What feelings erupt when I sin? Disgust? Frustration? Sadness? Anger? Guilt?

Do I ever think of myself as a prisoner of sin?

Have I ever really felt the power of gratitude?

A PRAYER

What shall I, a sinner, do?
Whither shall I turn for aid?
Conscience waking brings to view
Sins that make me sore afraid.
This my confidence shall be,
Jesus, I will cleave to thee.

JOHANN FLITNER (1618–1678),
FROM "WHAT SHALL I, A SINNER, DO?"

4

Why do I get so angry with God?

I know of a farmer who stayed angry with God because he wasn't "properly" rewarded for his efforts.

He was much like another man, a businessman who enjoyed great prosperity until his family was killed in a typhoon, his health failed, and he went bankrupt.

Expecting better, they both became exasperated with God.

A third man, a political leader in the Middle East, turned to God for help, but time and time again he threw up his hands in frustration. God seemed so slow.

All three of these men's stories are in the Bible. Cain. Job. David.

A couple from my church lost their young son in a car accident. They could not contain their rage against God.

Their names could have been yours or mine.

Anger against God is no small matter; at its deepest level it's grounded in the false belief that God is not good. When Cain expressed outrage,

God's first response was gentle and instructive; he understood Cain's limits (see Genesis 4).

God understands our limitations…like those of the grieving parents above. He understands that in a perfect world, none of us would ever get angry with him because we'd always know that he's good.

But he knows that it's not a perfect world.

He knows that we, too, will get frustrated with him, just like Job, who cried:

> I will give full vent to my complaint;
>   I will speak in the bitterness of my soul.
> I will say to God, "Do not condemn me;
>   Let me know why You contend with me.…
> According to Your knowledge I am indeed not guilty,
>   Yet there is no deliverance from Your hand." (Job 10:1–2, 7)

And he knows that we will shout like David:

> "How long, O LORD? Will You forget me forever?
>   How long will You hide Your face from me?" (Psalm 13:1)

Can you hear the exasperation—even anger—in their voices? Don't many of us feel that way sometimes?

Of course.

So why can't we "vent" too?

We can!

Job's and David's venting was not like Cain's. Cain's anger persisted because of disbelief in God's goodness. In contrast, Job and David demonstrated what I call "faithful frustration." They may have been agitated and even angry with God from time to time—their responses may not have been perfect—but they never turned against him. Why?

Because in spite of everything, they remembered *who God was* and that he was good.

Suffering Job made an inspiring remark: "Pity me, pity me, O you my friends, for the hand of God has struck me.... *[But] as for me, I know that my Redeemer lives*" (Job 19:21, 25).

And David finishes the jaw-clenched thirteenth psalm with a "but" of his own: "*But I have trusted in Your lovingkindness; my heart shall rejoice in Your salvation.*"

Life throws us all lots of curves. We have reasons to be angry with an all-powerful God who could make things different. But maybe the problem is not so much our *getting* angry with God as our *staying* angry with him.

We stay angry with God when we lose sight of who he is.

And why is this so easy to do? Speaking for myself, I lose sight of God on account of two tempting assumptions:

1. I assume I know how life should be.
2. I assume I know what God should do.

In effect, I see God in my own image.

That's because I'm arrogant...and I need to unload my persistent anger by confessing just that.

Like Job and David, we all have lots of reasons to wonder about God's ways. But confessing our pride and asking the Spirit to keep us mindful of who God is as our loving Father will help release us from that anger we feel. Then, like Job and David, we can go ahead and wrangle with God all we want. For God's grace sets us free to honestly vent our complaints with gusto…in faithful frustration.

Food for Thought

Is anger with God an undercurrent in my life?
What am I angry with him about?
What assumptions am I making about God?
What assumptions am I making about the way life "should" be?
How can I let go of my anger toward God?

A PRAYER

Though you slay me, Lord,
I will hope in you.
Though I love you, Lord,
I will argue my ways to your face.

ADAPTED FROM JOB 13:15

5

Why don't I have more faith?

Sister Margaret is a dear friend of mine from Britain who spent over thirty years as a Roman Catholic nun. Recently her monastic order dismissed her, rather cruelly, sending her back to the world homeless and nearly penniless. And yet a letter she sent me at the time shows her amazing resilience:

> Dear David,
>
> You ask what is faith in daily life? I don't know.
>
> But what I do know is that God is truly love and fidelity; that he loved us into being; that he is love.
>
> Pray for me, David, so that I may love him. For to lose intimacy with God would be worse than to live on the streets.

Billy Graham once said that faith can only exist in a world where faith is difficult. Well, our world qualifies as difficult, doesn't it? And when I look around, I realize just how difficult it is for me to flex my faith. I'm no Sister Margaret.

If we're honest, many of us are very well aware that we don't have much faith—that *active attitude* of confidence in the biblical witness.

We pray, but halfheartedly.

We worship, but with reservation.

We hope, but we're never quite convinced of in whom or what we can invest ourselves.

So what do we usually do?

At first, most of us try to excavate more faith out of our hearts. We dig deep into ourselves and try to *feel* something. We get real spiritual; we dive into devotions, Bible memory, small groups…but, alas…*nada*. We end up feeling like spiritual losers…again. So we forget the whole thing until life hits us in the face…again. Something's very wrong.

Do you remember the story of Peter walking on the water (Matthew 14:22–33)? As long as he was looking to Jesus he had all the faith he needed to stay dry. But when he turned to face the storm?

Soaked.

And do you remember the story of Jesus telling his bumbling disciples that if *they* had the faith of a mustard seed *they* could move mountains? I never liked that one because I always felt ashamed of not even having that little bit. But it eventually dawned on me that Jesus may have been teaching just the opposite of how the verse is often used. I think what he was saying just may be that we (like Peter and the crew) don't have *any* faith *apart from him*—otherwise all *we'd* need is a simple mustard seed's worth and we could move mountains and walk on water.

The truth is, faith doesn't come from us.

Now, here's where the "Calvary" shows up: "For by grace you have been saved through faith; and *that not of yourselves, it is the gift of God*" (Ephesians 2:8).

Faith in Christ is faith *from* Christ!

Faith is not something we muster up; faith is something we're given.

Instead of worrying about why *we* don't have more faith, we should take comfort in knowing that Christ Jesus has *all* the faith we'll ever need.

The better question, then, is why we don't experience more of *his* faith in our lives. And the answer is simple:

We forget to *ask*.

Like so many other things, we don't have because we don't ask. So instead of feeling like faith losers and instead of trying harder to do faith better, why don't we just come to Jesus—every day—and ask him to fill us with *his* faith. And like Sister Margaret, we may find we're able to face the storms of life faithfully after all.

Food for Thought

What is faith, anyway?

Do I have a deficit of faith?

How do I usually respond to the lack of faith I feel?

How does it feel to imagine that all the faith I need is available in Christ?

How would that awareness change me?

A PRAYER

We thank thee, then, O God of heaven,
That thou to us this faith hast given
In Jesus Christ thy Son, who is
Our only fount and source of bliss;
And from his fullness grant each soul
The rightful faith's true end and goal.

PETRUS HERBERT (1533–1571),
FROM "FAITH," *THE BRETHREN'S*
GERMAN HYMN BOOK, 1566

6

Why am I afraid to read my Bible?

A baggy-eyed Christian came up to me and blurted, "I'm afraid to read my Bible."

I stared at him for a long moment and then mumbled, "Uh, why?"

"Why?" He repeated the word with a hint of incredulity. "Well, if you knew my sins like I do, you'd be surprised I dare open the book at all."

His answer resonated with me. I nodded.

"But the good people at church are pretty insistent that I 'get into the Word' until I get things right."

"Yeah," I said. "But that's hard when all you find on the pages is shame."

His eyebrows abruptly arched. "You get it." He smiled. "You know, I've had more Bible verses hurled at me than dodge balls at a fat kid." He ground his fist into his palm. "It just doesn't help when they do that. Of course, they answer that the Spirit is convicting me, like he's using Scripture as an excruciating tool to torture my soul so that I'll finally 'surrender.'" He scuffed some dust in the air with his foot. "The truth is, the more I read God's words, the less I feel the love of God's Word. Anyway, that's why I'm afraid to read my Bible—and it's an uncomfortable admission."

Sometimes I'm afraid to read my Bible too.

Some of our churches have been clear in their instruction to dedicate time out of every day to read the Scriptures. We've been told to schedule daily devotions and to routinely commit verses to memory. That's a good thing.

But do you ever find yourself resolving to start, only to open "the Good Book" with dread?

Now, before I cause offense, I should go on record acknowledging my belief in the inspiration of Scripture and its critical importance in the life of any Christian. Its study is all too often ignored through indifference and laziness, leading to dangerous consequences. That said, the Bible has also been exploited as a weapon and a source of spiritual abuse, leading some to fear it.

So let me go way out on a limb and suggest that there are times we should *not* read our Bibles.

Some loving, kind, Spirit-filled counsel I received in a dark season of my own was from a Christian friend who told me to put my Bible down. "Don't open it for a long time," he said.

I was astonished.

My study of Koran

Now please understand, he didn't suggest this so that I could just wander off in my sin, nor that I might avoid the discomfort of correction. Quite the contrary, he knew I was in desperate need of the gospel.

But he had wisely recognized that I had been reading Scripture through a particular set of lenses.

The legalism I had been raised in had so clouded my vision that the gospel had been obscured from view.

Augustine made the bold point that if we read Scripture and don't see God's love, we have missed its proper meaning and failed to see truth.

Handicapped by poor instruction, I couldn't see God's love. What I needed was a season of prayer, time with the Spirit, and time with the counsel of those whose teaching bore the aroma of the Spirit's fruit. Later, with lenses partially cleared, I was able to return to Scripture and begin to see the Word, that is *Jesus,* in the words.

If you find that you are reluctant to read your Bible, set it aside and ask the Spirit to show you why you are afraid. And be wise to seek out the counsel of others whose lives are characterized by the Spirit's fruit—*for that is how we find where the gospel resides.*

Properly understood, Scripture is indeed "profitable for teaching, for reproof, for correction, for training in righteousness; so that the man [and woman] of God may be adequate, equipped for every good work" (2 Timothy 3:16–17).

May we be granted the eyes to see his grace and love on every page.

Food for Thought

Am I afraid, or have I ever been afraid, to read my Bible?

Do I sometimes make the Bible say what I think it should say?

What do I find more of in the Bible—angry commandments or merciful love?

Who in my life exhibits the fruits of the Spirit who might help point out to me God's love in the Scriptures?

A PRAYER

[Lord,] let me love my Bible more;
And take a fresh delight
By day to read these wonders o'er,
And meditate by night.

ISAAC WATTS (1674–1748),
FROM "GREAT GOD WITH WONDER
AND WITH PRAISE"

7

Why is loving others
so hard for me?

A number of years ago I knew a bitter man named Vernon who was nearly impossible to love. He was curt, demanding, and downright miserable.

One night lightning set his house on fire.

He screamed at the firemen and chased sympathetic neighbors away. He hated finding himself at the mercy of those he despised.

The next morning he stormed into a nearby café for breakfast. When finished, he demanded his check. The waitress pointed to a weary cook. "He paid it."

Vernon was dumfounded. "Why?"

"Dunno. But he said your house burned down. He's a fireman, you know. He didn't even get to bed last night."

Vernon met with me about six months later. He hung his head and confessed that he had spent his life keeping others out of his life. "I was wrong," he said.

* * * * * 25

As I listened, I thought about how I had avoided Vernon all the years I knew him. That made me uncomfortable. But though I was intrigued by his story, I had little interest in moving closer to him. He was just so hard to love.

And a month later, Vernon committed suicide.

Let's face it. Some people are hard to love; *we* may be hard to love. But as Christians we know that we're *supposed* to love others—and I'm not aware of any exceptions to that. Following Christ means loving the unlovable—as the cook did…as I didn't.

Others shouldn't need to be "qualified" for us to love them.

Unfortunately, many of us regularly disqualify certain people according to all sorts of standards. Do liberals, abortionists, or homosexuals feel "qualified" in many evangelical churches?

Why is it that so many of us find it hard to love the "others"? Do we feel superior? Do we want to avoid their issues? Are we afraid of them?

Probably.

But I wonder what else is going on. Mostly, I wonder if we've defined the love that Jesus calls us to as *feeling* love for them.

If so, we may find loving difficult because we have no *desire* to. Of course, the kind of love Jesus commands is actually agape love—at minimum a *behavior* of lovingness. So, I've heard a few preachers make loving easier by urging us to at least *do* love. And that seems to quiet a few consciences…even mine.

Fair enough.

But acting without feeling seems somehow incomplete to me.

It feels a little hypocritical, two-faced, insincere. I suppose we can grit our teeth from time to time and just *do* love. But is that kind of mechanical, dutiful witness really what Jesus had in mind? Were jaw-grinding "loving" acts what Jesus offered the unlovable of his world?

Why is it that we (I) have such little desire to love the hard to love?

In 1 John 4:19 we read, "We love, *because* He first loved us." It just may be that we don't *want* to love others because we've lost sight of Jesus's love for us. That's too bad, because remembering Jesus's love for us motivates us with gratitude and joy and a genuine *desire* to *be* loving—to *feel* loving—while doing love.

To be clear, acting lovingly without tender feeling can be a good thing, especially considering our human limitations. I'm simply suggesting that reconnecting feeling and behavior creates an even more powerful demonstration of love, one that's more authentic for the recipient.

So how do we do that? By appreciating Jesus's love for us more deeply.

We can bring our weaknesses, our failures, and our lack of love to Christ. And when he gives us better sight into his amazing grace, loving others *will* happen. And it will be easier—because that's what we'll *want* to do.

Food for Thought

Who do I find it difficult to love?
What would loving them look like?
Am I always easy to love?
When's the last time I explored Jesus's love for others?

A PRAYER

Lord, let me to others do,
As thou hast done to me,
Love them with love unfeigned and
*   true,*
Their servant be
Of willing heart, nor seek my own,
But as thou, Lord, hast helped us,
From purest love alone.

JUSTUS GESENIUS (1601–1673),
FROM "WHEN SORROW AND REMORSE"

8

Why do I so easily lose self-control?

Some years back I went on a day trip through the Amish farmlands with a couple and their unhappy toddler. We eventually stopped for dinner at a family-style restaurant, where we were seated at a long table.

The toddler scowled as she was jammed into her highchair.

The neighboring diners looked suddenly nervous.

The nice Mennonite servers began delivering hot plates of delicious food—but the toddler was not impressed. She began to cry.

Then she began to scream.

And scream.

And howl.

Finally, from somewhere across the room, a tourist with a Brooklyn accent, jumped to her feet and shrieked, "Shut that kid up!"

The room fell silent. For a moment the toddler was startled into silence.

I faced my plate and held my breath.

And the angry toddler pulled off one sandal and heaved it down the table and into a bowl of mashed potatoes.

Along life's journey I suspect most of us are sometimes the toddler and sometimes the shrieking patron. We lose control. We throw a fit.

Considering the temptations, disappointments, and obstacles of this world, self-control is often hard to come by.

But self-control is not just about temper tantrums.

Self-control is about controlling *Self.*

"Like a city that is broken into and without walls is a man who has no control over his spirit" (Proverbs 25:28). It is the self that tempts us into rebellion, into apathy, and toward the many idols life offers. The self has a gluttonous appetite and little interest in others. It creates the "me" culture around us.

Of course, its ultimate deception is *self*-righteousness. Self-righteousness turns us away from grace. It takes us off our knees and onto our feet so that we take the road leading away from the cross.

Is there anything more dangerous than that?

But what is the Self, anyway?

Ephesians 4 talks about the old self and the new self. The old self is who we are apart from our relationship with God; the new self is who we are as followers of Jesus. The self that needs controlling is the old self because it claims autonomy—independence from God.

But that Self is deceived.

The self is *not* independent; it's pressed on all sides by evil.

And evil will use the Self as a foothold to destroy us. The problem is, as long as we are on this side of heaven, followers of Jesus are not immune from the pressures of evil.

That's why the Self keeps trying to take control—and if it can, the Self will destroy us.

That's why the Scriptures urge us to be *self*-controlled…to be in control *of the Self.*

But how can I control *me*?

I can't.

It's like trying to see the back of my head without a second mirror. I can no more control my Self than I can see myself exactly as others do.

Bootstraps don't work…and neither does "bootstrap Christianity."

True self-control is too hard for us—and that's actually good news. The evil Self hates to hear this, but we are dependent creatures. We are created to need. And what we need is rescue. We need the Spirit to intervene. We need the Spirit to be the mirror to our selves. And we need the Spirit to enable us to control the Self we see there.

In Galatians 5:22–23 we learn that "the fruit of the Spirit is love, joy, peace, patience, kindness, goodness, faithfulness, gentleness, self-control."

Just like every other fruit, self-control *is a gift.* From the Giver.

And we would be wise to accept this gift, for the stakes are actually higher than we might think. Self-control is so much more than controlling temper tantrums. This is the danger we're actually in.

But a powerful gift is ours for the taking if we'd only ask.

Food for Thought

Do I have a lack of self-control in a particular area?

What does it usually look like?

How might self-control have changed a particular circumstance of mine?

In what other ways can my self be out of control?

How would a gift of the Spirit be different from control achieved by my own effort?

A PRAYER

O let thy Spirit's clear-eyed day
Break in upon our hearts' deep night,
And with its glowing radiance slay
Our self-trust's cold deluding light.

MARTIN OPITZ VON BOBERSFELD
(1597–1639), FROM "O LIGHT,
WHO OUT OF LIGHT WAST BORN"

9

Why do I fear unbelief?

In the course of writing this book, a sincere young woman named Linda admitted to me a terrible fear she suffered: she feared the consequences of not believing that many of the events described in the Bible actually happened.

She couldn't accept the idea of a six-day Creation—to her, the story just didn't make sense. Further, Linda couldn't believe that the whole world was drowned according to the story of Noah and the flood, or that the Red Sea parted. Nor could she swallow the story of Jonah and the great fish, or believe that an ax head floated (see 2 Kings 6), or that the sun was once held in place (see Joshua 10). I didn't even mention talking donkeys (see Numbers 22) and fire from heaven (see 1 Kings 18).

The New Testament had her struggling as well. Try as she might, she couldn't believe in the virgin birth, and she struggled terribly with the bodily resurrection of Jesus. But she did believe that Jesus is *the* way of forgiveness... She believed in the *message* of the Bible if not all its facts.

As a result, Linda feared she was going to hell.

After all, if she couldn't believe in an absolutely literal Bible, could she really be a Christian?

Wow.

First, I thanked her for saying out loud the kinds of things many in conservative churches secretly struggle with. Second, I reminded her that I have many more questions than answers.

But as we talked, my heart saddened all the more to see how fear weighed on her. She wasn't really struggling with how to believe in these hard-to-believe things but rather what that meant for her soul. She wanted so desperately to run into Jesus's open arms. But instead she faced a seemingly insurmountable wall of doctrines and belief requirements.

My mind flew to Matthew 18:6. "But whoever causes one of these little ones who believe in Me to stumble, it would be better for him to have a heavy millstone hung around his neck, and to be drowned in the depth of the sea."

Could it be that our various belief checklists have become unwitting stumbling blocks to Linda and those like her?

So what does it mean to believe in Jesus, anyway?

Does it mean believing in certain doctrines?

Does it mean accepting certain traditions?

Does "saving faith" equal trusting Jesus *plus* taking everything in the Bible as literal fact?

Correct doctrine is critical to every believer. But belief is not static, and we don't come upon it without significant soul-searching. Growing in sound doctrine helps sustain proper attitudes and behaviors and enriches our faith. I don't know if I could embrace true joy without accepting the bodily resurrection of Jesus. But doctrines vary among sincere believers; who's to say which ones constitute salvation?

Tradition is incredibly valuable too. In it we find the wisdom of those who have journeyed before us. But traditions vary—and what does that mean for Linda?

How critical it is to appreciate Scripture for all it is. It is our supreme written authority, which points us to Jesus and his love. But who can deny the honest differences among Christians in the way the Bible is to be understood?

Here is what I know: Salvation is found in believing in Jesus alone. Plus nothing. And belief in Jesus as Savior is perhaps best understood as "beloving" Jesus.

Only God knows for sure, but I'm pretty sure that Linda be-loves Jesus: she believes that he *is*, and she has received him into her being. *Linda loves Jesus; Jesus loves Linda.* That's the wonder of childlike faith. She is a believer…a belover—a follower of Jesus. That's awesome news for a fearful soul.

"But as many as received Him, to them He gave the right to become children of God, even to those who believe in His name" (John 1:12).

Food for Thought

What does "believing in Jesus" mean to me?
Have I added any belief requirements to my trust in Jesus?
What other requirements have I had to denounce?
What would I have said to Linda?
Do I think that Linda is a believer?

A PRAYER

Thou art my hiding-place, O Lord,
In thee I put my trust;
Encouraged by thy holy word,
A feeble child of dust:
I have no argument beside,
I urge no other plea;
And 'tis enough my Savior died,
My Savior died for me.

THOMAS RAFFLES (1788–1863), FROM
"THOU ART MY HIDING-PLACE, O LORD"

10

Why am I so afraid of death?

When I was a little boy I had quite a fright. My parents took me to visit a great-aunt, an elderly woman who lay dying in an upstairs bedroom.

The house was scary. Its wallpaper was musty and faded, and the woodwork was dark. Creaking staircases led to spooky Victorian towers, and noises came from the cellar. But deciding to test my mettle, I sneaked away from the kitchen conversation and slowly climbed the stairs leading to a shadowy corridor through which I carefully crept.

Suddenly the old woman emerged from a dark doorway, ghost-like and terrifying. Her white hair flowed over the shoulders of a long, white gown. Her yellowed eyes could not have been wider than my own. My mouth opened but I couldn't scream.

Startled, the woman froze in place until the hall clock chimed. That's when she leaned toward me and whispered, "David, I am so afraid of the G-R-A-V-E."

I bolted.

⁂

Thinking back on it, I believe this may be why I'm afraid of dying *and* secretly claustrophobic. I can see the tight dirt walls closing in on me. I'm envious of those who have no such concerns. But as a Christian I feel guilty for being afraid of anything, especially death. Where's my faith hiding?

I hope not in that old house because there's no way I'm going back!

Paul boldly wrote, "O death, where is your sting?" (1 Corinthians 15:55).

Good for Paul.

David wrote, "Even though I walk through the valley of the shadow of death, I fear no evil, for You are with me" (Psalm 23:4).

Good for David.

I'm still scared.

The fact is, unlike the very faithful, I do fear death, and I have a hunch many others do too. The question is, why?

Well, why not?

We weren't made to die.

We were made to live eternally. So I don't buy the line that "death is natural." It isn't. God created the world to *live*. And so I abhor death. When those I love die, I cry. I weep when I bury my pets. When gazelles are torn to bits by lions on television, I'm saddened. The whole realm of death is dark and horrible.

Death is our enemy, and I think it's good to call it what it is.

But death *is* a fact of life, and there's no escaping it. So what do we do?

First, let's not feel ashamed. *Fear* of death seems pretty natural. Death is a great mystery from which no one I've ever met has recovered.

So we're left with three choices: we can deny our fears, rationalize them, or admit them.

I've decided to admit mine. That doesn't make me brave, but I've learned that it's often easier than the alternatives. Besides, I find it liberating.

Admitting something is like expelling poison.

And when we do it, we take in something quite different: relief.

Admissions like this are really confessions. After all, fear of death really is grounded in a lack of faith. The Bible makes it very plain that death has been overcome by Christ's Resurrection and that heaven is our destiny. But plain or not, some fears are hard to overcome, and confession is the first step in turning them over to God. It's a way of handing him our burdens—which is exactly what he invites us to do.

Confession of fears helps replace them.

Why is that? "There is no fear in love; but perfect love casts out fear" (1 John 4:18). God tells us earlier in that same chapter that life in Christ brings the promise of confidence, *even confidence in death.* Confessing to him fears of death allows his love to replace such fear with confidence.

So I will ask him to walk closer to me, to hear my confessions, to replace my fears with the confidence of his love. And in time, I hope to join Paul and David and lift my chin against death, reinforced by faith.

Food for Thought

Do I or others I know fear death?

How can I find more faith to overcome my fear?

How does love cast out fear?

As a Christian, is it okay to have fears?

How could confessing my fear strengthen my relationship
with Jesus?

A PRAYER

With peace and joy I now depart;
God's child I am with all my heart.
I thank thee, Death, thou leadest me
To that true life where I would be.
So cleansed by Christ I fear not death.
Lord Jesus, strengthen thou my faith.

PAUL EBER (1511–1569), FROM "I FALL
ASLEEP IN JESUS'S WOUNDS"

11

Why am I so confused about finding God's will?

My mother's family were (and some still are) Pennsylvania Mennonites. They picked their pastors by something called "the lot"—prayerfully drawing names, based on the selection of Matthias to replace Judas in Acts 1. The congregation was rightly concerned to follow God's leading in their selection.

A dear friend of mine used weather conditions, like Gideon used fleeces in Judges 6. She was trying to discern God's will for her choice of college.

Another friend prayed that if God wanted him to buy a certain car, God would need to have a certain person say a certain word before lunch.

I used to agonize over all sorts of decisions, fearing that the wrong one would put me on God's *permissive* path (second best) rather than his *perfect* path (first choice).

Without sounding judgmental, some of this sounds…well, is superstitious too strong a word?

Seeking God's will is what a child of God should want very much to do. That's what letting him be the "potter" and us the "clay" is really all about. But something doesn't feel right about throwing feathers in the air, listening for secret codes on the radio, or claiming rainbows.

Yet in my life I've sometimes been paralyzed by uncertainty about what God wants me to do, like which college to choose, which house to buy, where to go on vacation, what book to write, where to go for dinner...

So I've sought all sorts of ways to find answers, including some mentioned above.

But it all seems fear based and burdensome.

Something feels wrong.

It seems to me that this idea of "finding God's will for my life" has somehow been turned into a kind of get-it-right-or-else process, when actually God's will is simply *God's desire.*

And if we want to know what that is, he already told us in Matthew 22:37–39: love God and love your neighbor. And he points us to some ways of doing that: "Rejoice always; pray without ceasing; in everything give thanks; *for this is God's will for you in Christ Jesus*" (1 Thessalonians 5:16–18).

That's no surprise. We get that.

The problem is that we confuse the idea of "finding God's will" with making a godly decision. And the difference is important.

God's will is already revealed.

Figuring out how to make it happen is something else entirely.

And for that we need to explore a different question: how do I find wisdom?

"But if any of you lacks wisdom, let him ask of God, who gives to all generously and without reproach, and it will be given to him" (James 1:5).

Ask. What a concept! Once again, it's all about him—even making decisions. For me, that's a relief. No more obsessing about playing hide-and-seek with God's will.

Now, I'm not one for formulas, but I have found three things to do that have been helpful in my (sometimes poor) decision-making process over the years:

- Pray for wisdom.
- Seek the counsel of others I trust.
- Seek the guidance of the Scriptures.

In so doing, I've learned to abandon my fears of making a wrong decision and just depend on the One who ultimately "wills my will," that is, molds my desires (see Philippians 2:13). He has set me free to make my own decisions wisely. This means I can make decisions boldly. After praying, seeking counsel, and checking Scripture, I really am free to hold my nose and jump!

Of course, sometimes our freedom will lead us into a decision that disappoints or hurts. But is God not sovereign over all things? Can't he redeem a sincerely wrong choice into something good? Does that mean we were "out of his will"?

No.

As long as we're asking him for wisdom and guidance, let's never be afraid of messing things up.

The truth is, when we know he's in charge, we can't.

Food for Thought

Have I been afraid of missing God's will for my life?

What does that concept really mean to me?

Do I understand the difference between finding God's will and decision making?

What is wisdom?

How do I know when I've found it?

A PRAYER

Guide me, O thou great Jehovah,
Pilgrim through this barren land.
I am weak, but thou art mighty;
Hold me with thy powerful hand.

WILLIAM WILLIAMS (WILLIAMS OF PANTYCELYN) (1717–1791), FROM "GUIDE ME, O THOU GREAT JEHOVAH"

12

Why am I so angry?

I was in a long line at the customer service counter of a large retail store the other day. At the front were a mother and two children. The children were screaming at each other. Instead of completing her transaction, the mother threw her returns on the floor and began shouting at her kids. The line began to grumble, and someone behind me started sending snide remarks forward.

Once the kids were finally under control, the mother turned her fury against the frustrated clerk, who abruptly decided she'd had enough. She fired off a few choice words, then grabbed the wall phone and barked through the store intercom for a supervisor.

It was all rather amusing…but not really funny.

Anger is a natural human emotion. And emotions are neither good nor bad in themselves. Sometimes we have good reasons to get angry. Anger can be a reaction to injustice, it can express passion for those we love and for sound beliefs we hold dear. Even God gets angry—and you and I are made in his image.

It's the beliefs that drive the feelings that we need to be concerned with.

And when we find ourselves living in a constant state of anger, something's probably wrong. That's when our belief system has us blowing up at people, blurting out ultimatums, snapping, biting, and hurling hurtful words—or worse.

Of course not everyone shows their anger the same way. Some of us don't actually erupt. We may not blow our stacks, but we seethe underneath. We're the ones who leak our anger out in sarcasm, rolled eyes, shaking heads, and clipped conversation.

Then there are those among us who never let anger out, so we face heart disease, high blood pressure, depression, and other stress-related illnesses.

Does any of this look like godly anger? Does it seem related to the example of Jesus?

We need to be aware of two kinds of anger: godly and ungodly.

When Jesus angrily threw over the moneychangers' tables (see John 2:14–17), his disciples recognized his zeal. The same holds true for those times he angrily confronted the Pharisees. Jesus was zealous for truth; he was defending others. His anger was indeed godly.

I'm afraid most of us are not typically angry for the cause of truth or the welfare of others. I'm not. Unlike Jesus's anger, I'm afraid my anger is usually for the cause of me…and all too often I believe in myself more than in truth.

It's when my anger is serving my purposes that it's ungodly.

Too often I demand what *I* want; I demand to look good, feel good, control events, control others, and satisfy my expectations. My pride drives me. So when I don't get what I assume I should, I'm disappointed.

And pride-driven disappointment is what leads to ungodly anger.

Knowing this can be helpful in uncomfortable situations. When facing an angry person, I try to imagine *what is disappointing* them. Have I let them down? Are circumstances not going the way they wanted? What has thwarted their desires?

When I'm angry, I ask the same questions, praying for the Spirit to open my eyes to my selfish demands.

Living in a state of anger is a prison. It warps our attitudes, it ruins relationships, it interferes with joy, peace, and all the other wonderful gifts of a Spirit-led life. Paul reminds us that "it was for freedom that Christ set us free" (Galatians 5:1). That freedom includes freedom from ungodly anger.

Food for Thought

Do I think of myself as an angry person?

Do others ever think of me that way?

What disappointments am I currently facing? Are those tied to selfish or Spirit-led desires?

Who in my life seems angry? Am I aware of what disappointments they are struggling with?

A PRAYER

You withdrew all Your fury;
You turned away from Your burning
    anger.
Restore us, O God of our salvation,
And cause Your indignation toward us
    to cease....
Will You not Yourself revive us again,
That Your people may rejoice in You?
Show us Your lovingkindness, O LORD,
And grant us Your salvation.

PSALM 85:3–4, 6–7

13

Why can't I seem to "run the good race"?

At a family reunion, my then seven-year-old son entered a three-legged race. When the whistle blew, he and his buddy took their first step only to tumble in a tangled heap. Giggling wildly, they helped each other to their feet and tried again, this time getting a little farther before laughing the whole way to the finish line.

The same son joined his ninth-grade cross-country team. He didn't laugh once; he hated it! I remember watching him race one particular rainy day in April. I stood under my umbrella at the edge of a clearing, waiting patiently for him to dash by. He finally emerged from the dripping woods, all alone and splattered with mud.

I cheered him on, but he slanted a desperate sideways look that I heard in my head. "Dad, this really stinks."

Drawing on the popularity of races in ancient times, several passages in the New Testament compare the Christian life to running a race. In 1 Corinthians 9:24, Paul urges us to "run in such a way that you may win."

Jesus need - "I'm doing the best I can!"

The problem is, many Christians I know (myself included) sometimes feel that running the good race is another demand we just can't satisfy. Many of us have had preachers and Sunday school teachers interpret running as performing for God.

So we get out there and try harder—we become high-performance runners.

And we're told what "running better" looks like: regular devotions, more prayer time, living "victoriously," ad nauseam.

Unfortunately, the tragic effect of performance running is lots of exhausted, discouraged, confused, and angry Christians. We look very much like my son on his cross-country race.

And some quit the race altogether.

Is this the image of the Christian life that Jesus or Paul envisioned?

If so, we should all be issued some kind of logo for our sweatbands—maybe a swoosh-style cross or a dove with jet engines under its wings. But what if running the Christian race is not about mustering more willpower? What if running has nothing to do with performing better?

What if running the good race is about something else?

It's interesting to me that the verse just ahead of the 1 Corinthians verse reads, "I do all things *for the sake of the gospel.*" What if running the good race means simply living the gospel?

What *is* living the gospel?

The Bible is the story of humankind's weakness. It's about our *inability* to perform and God's love for us anyway. The truth is, living the gospel has nothing to do with *our* performance and everything to do with *Jesus.*

Living the gospel means running *by faith;* running the good race means we're faith runners.

And faith is the opposite of performance.

Faith means letting go of our self-reliance—acknowledging our *inability* to run well on our own—and binding our legs to Christ. The writer of Hebrews offers us encouragement: "Let us run with endurance [patience] the race that is set before us, fixing our eyes on Jesus, *the author and perfecter of faith*" (Hebrews 12:1–2).

The victory, like the race itself, belongs to Christ.

Running by faith is more like my son's three-legged race than his lonely cross-country one. Yes, we may stumble and we may trip, but we are tied to Jesus. He invites us to delight in dashing boldly with him through an abundant life of joy. And ultimately, it's he who will carry us over the finish line—and all we have to do to wear the victor's crown is trust that!

Food for Thought

What comes to mind when I hear the expression "run the good race"?

What characterizes "winning" Christianity?

Have I felt guilty for not running well? What was it that made me feel guilty?

How can I run well as a Christian and not try to achieve success in my own strength?

A PRAYER

Guide us, Lord, from day to day,
Keep us in the paths of grace,
Clear all hindrances away
That might foil us in the race!
When we stumble hear our call,
Work repentance for our fall.

JOACHIM NEANDER (1650–1680),
FROM "COME, O COME,
SPIRIT OF LIFE"

14

Why does God seem
silent in my life?

I recently read an article by a theologian who insisted that God does not speak. She thought the whole idea was ridiculous, since God has no vocal cords. "For crying out loud," I said with smug contempt. "Of course he doesn't have a larynx!"

But then I set the article on my lap and realized that God often seems silent in my life. He suddenly seemed like an imaginary friend whom I talk to but who never answers. *Sure,* I said to myself. *I write about him, talk to him, wait on him…but nothing seems to come the other way. He doesn't show me his face; I don't feel his touch; I don't hear his voice.*

So I looked out my window and wondered if the theologian was right after all. I asked myself if God really is silent—or does it just seem like he is?

We know that God "speaking" in our lives is a metaphor for seeing evidence of him and experiencing his presence. When we say he seems silent, we probably mean that we don't *experience* him.

And that's a shame for us, for that sense of abandonment can lead to unhealthy doubt, distance, and sometimes disbelief.

And why not? It's not easy for sane people to speak with someone who doesn't talk back.

So what's really going on? Is God really silent?

The Bible is packed with references to God speaking to his prophets and through his creation. "Let the earth rejoice; let the sea roar.… Let the field exult.… Then all the trees of the forest will sing for joy" (Psalm 96:11–12). But the psalmist also said this: "Oh that My [God's] people would *listen* to Me" (81:13).

Hmm. It occurs to me that my sense of not experiencing God may not be about God at all. It may be about me.

I may need to rethink my idea of listening.

A friend of mine in Scotland angrily waited on Jesus for a response to her suffering. Finally, as she put it, "He asked me to tell him about the beauty of the day. I choked out a bit about the poppies and then went right back to the rage.

"He gently accepted the poppies and then asked me a bit more about the beauty of the day… I sighed and did just that until gradually my strongest awareness was of his love."

As I think of her story, I realize that God is *not* silent, but rather he offers his voice in ways I too often neglect. It just may be that if I listen differently, he's there waiting for me to experience him in:

- creation
- the Bible
- being Jesus to others
- impressions of the Spirit

- others themselves
- silence

Ironically, silence can be one of the greatest means of experiencing God. "Be still, and know that I am God" (Psalm 46:10, NIV) is an invitation for us to hear God in the quiet places. For in stillness, the noise of the world gives way.

And when the world is set aside, God emerges.

But how do we know when we are hearing (experiencing) God? It's a good question. So much around us is just images and chatter.

How do we listen for God?

God is love. We listen for God by listening for love.

And love waits for us to notice her in beauty and in wisdom, in Word and words, in song and deed...beyond us and from the Spirit within us. So why not begin to open our awareness to the *experience* of love that permeates all that is? For when we experience love, we have heard the voice of God.

And by this we will know that God is not silent in our lives at all.

Food for Thought

What am I listening *for*?

What am I listening *to*?

What do I expect to hear?

Are my ideas of experiencing God's presence too
limited?

Has God spoken to me in ways I haven't noticed?

A PRAYER

How silently, how silently,
The wondrous gift is given!
So you impart to human hearts
The blessings of your heaven.
No ears may hear your coming,
But in our world of sin,
Where meek souls will receive you still,
Dear Jesus, enter in.

ADAPTED FROM "O LITTLE TOWN
OF BETHLEHEM," PHILLIPS BROOKS
(1835–1893)

15

Why do I avoid sharing my faith?

Ian, one of my colleagues at divinity school, posted an intriguing message one day:

> To All,
>
> I just put a sticky note in an area of high visibility in my home that reads, "The greatest need of those around me is my personal holiness."
>
> Blessings, Ian

I understood the sentiment, but I asked Ian to define personal holiness. He answered, "Consistent Christlikeness. But so you don't think I'm a legalist, I live according to what Jesus would *do* and I don't focus so much on the *don'ts*."

"Just so I understand," I wrote back, "your Christlike living is the *greatest need* others have?"

"Yes, that's the most important way we can invite them to have Christ in their own lives."

I'm afraid there are lots of reasons many of us fear sharing our faith. Sometimes we may feel embarrassed, or maybe we're afraid that we might not have the right answers for hard questions.

But Ian's posting made me wonder if I often avoid sharing my faith because I don't feel "qualified." Is my personal holiness really a prerequisite for sharing the gospel?

Let's forget all the other issues that this brief exchange could open and concentrate on Ian's idea of witnessing. How do you feel when you're told that your Christlikeness is the *most important* way to share your faith?

Are you encouraged?

Excited?

Relieved?

Enabled?

Ian's approach discourages me. It sets a standard that I don't keep very well. It's as if "right living" once again qualifies and disqualifies Christians—this time from inviting others to Jesus.

Now, if you're like me...one who's more like Paul in Romans 7 (doing the don'ts and not doing the dos) than Jesus, this is just the sort of thing that may leave you feeling substandard, embarrassed, or too hypocritical to share the gospel.

The sad truth is, we Christ-ians (little Christs) rarely behave according to who we are...not even Ian does, despite his intentions.

Whether we like it, admit it, or even see it, we strugglers are far from being Christlike, and that's been the story since the beginning.

Think about it.

Paul couldn't get along with Mark, the Corinthian church was infamously immoral, other churches were beset by dissention and jealousies… Yet they shared their faith anyway and changed the world.

How did they do it?

Instead of focusing on Christlikeness, they focused on Christ.

Instead of pointing to Christ *as* them, they pointed to Christ *in* them.

Jesus shows us what people need most from us. They need us to love them *as they are,* even as we show them Christ's love for us *as we are.* So he instructs us to remove the logs from our own eyes first (see Luke 6:41–42), to humble ourselves before others as witness to God's love of the weak, the broken, and the shamed. That's why Paul exposed himself as the "chief" (KJV) or "foremost of all" sinners (1 Timothy 1:15). That's how we *un*-Christlike hypocrites can talk credibly about his love and his forgiveness, his acceptance, and his unconditional favor on us.

It's when we admit our *lack* of personal holiness that others may just get a glimpse of Christ in us.

So relax a little, Christian. Your story is what it is: one fractured by inconsistencies but also made whole by grace. Your story *is* the gospel at work—and hearing your story as it really is inspires others toward the truth of Christ's love for them.

Of course we should live as much like Jesus as we can. But when we fail, we need to tell that part of the story too. We need to just keep on telling our story—scary parts and all.

Food for Thought

How many different things keep me from sharing my faith?
Do any of them make sense?
Do others feel the same way?
How can these obstacles be overcome?
Why is it hard to tell my whole story?

A PRAYER

*Lord of all in heaven and on earth, hear
     me, a sinner who is also your child.
Lion of Judah, forgive me of my many
     weaknesses, and grant me peace.
Lover of my soul, shine through me in spite
     of all that needs forgiveness in my life,
And may I be an instrument of your mercy.*

16

Why am I so discontented?

Jeanne was the high school class president, graduated magna cum laude from the state university, is an accomplished cellist who played second chair in a metropolitan orchestra for a few years, and is a black belt in karate. She is married and has three children, two of which are active participants in a variety of sports, clubs, and the like. Recently Jeanne got her pilot's license and announced plans to open a small restaurant once her youngest child is off her hip.

Jeanne is generally agitated.

Randy is a local insurance agent who takes clients to every home game of the Philadelphia Eagles (football), most of the Flyers games (hockey), and quite a few of the Phillies (baseball). He strives day and night to win every company sales award. He coaches soccer for both his sons with a cell phone in his ear, is an avid but badly distracted golfer (hence the hooks), and feels obliged to teach Sunday school.

Randy doesn't smile much.

I like to fish. At least I did until I found myself on a boat with two friends who were sound asleep while I was standing at the bow with a rod in each hand. Sit in the sun and doze? Relax? Enjoy the gentle bob of the boat? Not on your life!

I'm too intense.

All three of us are discontented.

Now I'm quite sure God has blessed some among us with an unusual treasure trove of talents and energy that has them bubbling with optimism. For them, the world is a gift of new horizons. They leap from bed with a dream and a smile, and they make things happen. Good for them.

Then there are the rest of us.

We're the ones others call "driven." We can usually be spotted by the way we push our shopping carts through stores or the way we don't listen well and how we pace while on the phone. Some of us sport dark circles under our eyes, mouth-breathe, and make sure we're always near noise.

We are not at peace. We're itchy.

We might describe ourselves with some of the following conditions:

- unhappy but not sure why
- dissatisfied but not sure why
- fearful but not sure why
- having unreasonable expectations
- disappointed by life
- having an exaggerated sense of responsibility
- suppressing true feelings
- needing to impress
- desperate for affirmation

- confused by life
- running from the past
- having low self-esteem

Some of us may have understandable reasons for being like this that could fill lots of books. But underneath it all I suspect we'd find some complicated, monstrous demon of pain or desire that's chasing us, demanding that *something* be satisfied. We may not even know what... We only see the symptoms.

In Philippians 4:11 Paul wrote, "Not that I speak from want, *for I have learned* to be content in whatever circumstances I am." Paul *learned* contentment.

But how on earth can we learn to be content?

Confessing our states of mind to Christ is all we can do—that and realizing we really don't *have* to be running, trying, hiding, pushing. All we need is to remember to rest in Christ. Jesus is already obsessed with our welfare. He says, "Come to Me, all who are weary and heavy-laden, and I will give you rest" (Matthew 11:28).

Rest.

Some of us are so discontented we look right past rest and toward the next objective. But there's a healthier way to live.

Jesus shows us how to be contented and whole. That's how we'll enjoy him, face trials in peace, and love others well. He wants to help us believe that all we really need is him.

That's the truth that Paul learned—and contentedness followed.

Food for Thought

Do I consider myself discontented?

What makes me feel relaxed, at peace?

Is my contentedness circumstance driven?

How does my intensity affect others? How does it affect me?

A PRAYER

[O Lord,] let me learn to abound,
Let me learn to suffer need,
In whatsoever state I am,
Therewith to be content.

BISHOP LANCELOT ANDREWES (1555–
1626), FROM "PRAYER FOR GRACE"

17

Why is my conscience
so sensitive?

I received a letter from a reader of my book *101 Cups of Water* that made me very sad.

Dear David,

I have a really sensitive conscience, but I think it's distorting my view of God. I obsess about everything I enjoy because I'm afraid it might be a sin. I threw away all my music and magazines that aren't from Christian publishers. I gave up my playhouse tickets and bowling. I feel guilty for enjoying them; I feel guilty for wanting them back.

Some of my family got sick and one died. Now I can't help but wonder if God is punishing me. I've given up on the Bible because I feel like I'm supposed to understand everything and it's just too hard. Something's not right.

Blessings,

Sandy

One of the many tragedies surrounding Sandy's letter is that she's not alone. Many who have followed moralism instead of Christ suffer the same kind of hypervigilant conscience that distracts them from their liberty and from loving Jesus.

But doesn't conscience keep sin in check? Doesn't the conscience protect us?

Okay, but what is the conscience, anyway?

The conscience is an inner "voice"—a faculty of our being that guides us in deciding right and wrong. And that's worth paying attention to because *some of us confuse the conscience with the Spirit.*

Just because we feel our conscience pricking us doesn't mean it should.

The conscience is *human.*

And like every other member of our being, the conscience is imperfect.

That means the conscience can go "rogue." It can step out of bounds; it can make us serve a different master.

But how can we tell when something's not right?

I think the answer may be back in the idea of "voice." Our consciences are voices. Powerful ones. But whose?

The question is critically important. Whomever our consciences speak for is our master.

Some consciences speak for an angry parent. Some for a controlling pastor. Some for a community of false teaching.

And some speak for the Spirit.

So how can we tell whose voice is speaking?

We listen, carefully.

We listen by pausing to ask ourselves if our consciences are responding to Scripture.

And we pause to ask how we feel when our consciences speak. Do we feel accused? condemned? overwhelmed by shame?

If so, the voice we're hearing is not the Spirit's.

Satan condemns us, not the Spirit (see Revelation 12).

And when Satan gains a stronghold in our conscience, his voice becomes louder and louder. The accusations become deafening, and we end up seeking the approval of the accuser's voice by obeying his twisted notions of good and bad. That's why poor Sandy's life was being destroyed.

So how do we let the Spirit become the master of our conscience again?

We pray for sight to see the Scriptures more clearly, and we pray for help in remembering the joy of the gospel: "There is now no condemnation for those who are in Christ Jesus" (Romans 8:1).

And we listen for the Spirit. The Spirit will show us our sins, not to accuse us but to teach us and remind us of how much we have been forgiven.

The Spirit uses healthy consciences to restore us to joy and to protect us by teaching us what real sin looks like.

So what do real sins look like?

Gossip? Pride? Hate? Sure.

Bowling? Beethoven? *Good Housekeeping*? Not normally. If our conscience keeps defaulting to "*nothing* is lawful," we can be pretty sure the accuser is back.

The Spirit's desire for us is freedom; liberty is the voice of grace... and that's the only voice worth hearing.

Food for Thought

Does my conscience have power in my life?
When's the last time my conscience spoke to me?
Did it point me to freedom or to bondage?
Does my conscience steal my joy?
Does it feel like a helper or an enemy?

A PRAYER

Dear Shepherd... within these walls
let holy peace
And love, and concord dwell;
Here give the troubled conscience ease,
The wounded spirit heal.

JOHN NEWTON (1725–1807), FROM
"O LORD, OUR LANGUID SOULS INSPIRE"

18

Why do I only pray in emergencies?

When I was a boy, I loved to watch professional wrestling on television. That's the crazy sporting event where huge men pretend to pound the life out of each other.

One of my favorite matches was the tag team. Each wrestler had a partner who would stand outside the ropes as a backup. When a wrestler was almost beaten, he'd stretch his hand out and tap his partner's. Then the partner would come in and crush the opponent.

That's how I usually think of prayer. I'm the wrestler fighting with life; the Holy Spirit is my partner just beyond the ropes. When I can't take any more, I reach for him.

Now, I realize prayer should be different than a tag-team match, but if I'm honest, prayer is usually my *last* option—the one after everything else goes wrong.

Why is that?

"Pray without ceasing" was Paul's command in 1 Thessalonians 5:17. It seems straightforward enough. But do I? Do we?

Well…I don't.

Is it because I don't really believe prayer makes a difference? Or do I think God isn't really listening? Do I doubt his interest in the humdrum of my daily life? Does it seem like too much effort?

Sometimes.

But I think the main reason I pray last is because I imagine I can handle most things on my own.

And I'm pretty sure many of us think like that.

Why? It may be that we've bought into ideas of self-sufficiency. We're taught by our culture to be independent minded. And we've been taught in churches (probably unwittingly) that life functions according to a partnership of sorts: we do our part and the Holy Spirit does his. So life becomes something of a "God helps those who help themselves" thing.

With the Holy Spirit reduced to a "partner," we instinctively approach a problem by looking to our own strengths first.

And when we successfully overcome some situation without "bothering" to pray, we feel pretty good about ourselves. At least I do. And feeling good about ourselves is a very powerful motivator.

But when we (I) fail in life, we usually do turn to prayer. Yet strange as it seems, that can make some of us actually feel ashamed. In a weird way, having to pray becomes an admission of failure…and that's awfully hard to do without feeling ashamed.

I can't help but wonder if we've missed the whole idea of prayer because we've missed the real nature of our relationship with Christ.

Instead of a partnership, we are in union with Christ (see Galatians 2:20).

Understanding that better might actually begin to change our whole idea of prayer. Union is like a relationship between spouses or the closest of friends in which a mingling of identities occurs. Words aren't always exchanged, but there is a conscious awareness of the other. Prayer is this kind of engagement, a state of union that *leaves no room for self-sufficiency.*

Understood as communion with God, prayer is never a first, second, or last option... It isn't an *option* at all.

It just is.

Our lives become prayers.

That's because every event, decision, reaction, hope, or disappointment in life is awash in union with him... One who sometimes uses words and is sometimes silent but is always exchanging thanksgivings or requests, sharing joys or fears. Prayer is no longer some special act that taps into "his part" to help "our part."

Instead, prayer becomes a state of being with the Spirit and us engaging life as one.

To me, this is "praying without ceasing."

Now, if I could get my prideful, self-reliant self out of the way, I might actually experience the joy of union with him. And prayer would become the automatic, uninterrupted connection with the One with whom I dwell.

This suddenly sounds like a way of life worth praying for!

Food for Thought

Am I aware of why and when I pray?
Are there things I do and don't pray about?
When is prayer difficult?
When is prayer easy?
What difference does prayer make in my sense of who
God is to me?

A PRAYER

O Lord, keep us unafraid to pray, for
to pray is right.
Let us pray, if we can, with hope, but
ever praying
Even if hope be weak.
Whatever is good to wish, help us ask
that of heaven.
Help us, Lord, be unafraid to pray.

ADAPTED FROM "PRAYER," HARTLEY
COLERIDGE (1796–1849)

19

Why is my life such a mess?

Art was the favored twin growing up. So ever since he was a child, Art had been accustomed to having all that he wanted.

He was good-looking and smart, clever and personable. As an adult he married his sweetheart, succeeded in business, and was important in any number of life categories.

Ultimately, what he wanted was to feel respected, important, and comfortable. To do that, he began trying to impress others with his cars, house, and expensive parties. He ran up his credit cards and re-mortgaged his house to the max. His marriage felt the strain. In time and for lots of reasons, Art divorced his wife, lost his job, and eventually declared bankruptcy. Panicked and suffering anxiety, he sought comfort in red wine—gallons of it. By the time he was fifty he was broke, alone, and diabetic. Art's life was a mess.

Individual lives can be messy for all sorts of reasons. The prom queen turns into a junky; the top salesman goes bust; perfect marriages crash and burn. Sometimes it's about our choices or our reactions to circumstances. Sometimes it's about our assumptions and beliefs. Sometimes it's all the above.

But underneath our lives lay our hearts…home for a tricky thing called *desire.*

Our hearts tell us what we want.

Unfortunately, all too often the things we want are at cross-purposes with what's good for us and for those we love. That's when we end up with a mess…like Art.

It's *critical* that we pause from time to time to take a heart test—to ask ourselves what it is we really *want* out of life.

How our hearts answer will tell us what we love.

And what we love determines how we live.

So how do we test our hearts' desires?

We might want to begin by asking the Spirit to show us our hearts. "Search me, O God, and know my heart" (Psalm 139:23). If we do, we better brace ourselves. It might get real ugly real fast!

And we also should pay attention to how God made us. We are created with four primary needs that motivate us every day. They are:

- significance—the need to matter
- identity—the need to know who we are
- security—the need to feel safe
- relief of pain—the need to feel well

When we find ourselves in some sort of life mess, we can be pretty sure that at least one of these needs has impacted our desires. The need for significance can make us obsessive achievers. Identity crises can lead to unhealthy associations. Security concerns can create chronic fear. Pain relief can drive us to addictions. All these things put us at cross-purposes with the kind of healthy living that God wants for us.

But we do have ways to keep these natural needs in check:

- We need to rediscover Cross-purposes.
- We need to want what he wants for us.

Of course, we are not created with the power to change our own desires. But we can ask the Spirit to begin changing our wants. And, importantly, we can ask the Spirit to help us better appreciate how it is that the things we need *are already provided for* in Christ!

In him we are *already:*

- Significant: we are promised the kingdom (see James 2:5). What could be more impressive than that!
- Identified: we are declared "children of God" (Romans 8:16). Talk about a title!
- Secure: "The one who comes to Me I will certainly not cast out" (John 6:37). Need I say more?
- Relieved of pain: Actually, no. But we are *not abandoned* to pain. "For just as the sufferings of Christ are ours in abundance, so also our comfort is abundant through Christ" (2 Corinthians 1:5).

Yes, I am a mess.

You may be a mess.

But praise God, Jesus is not and we are in him.

Food for Thought

What would make my life seem like less of a mess?
What have I tried to do in the past to fix my messes?
What makes me feel significant or secure?
Do I struggle with identity?
How do I relieve my pain?

A PRAYER

Create in me a clean heart, O God,
And renew a steadfast spirit within me....
Restore to me the joy of Your salvation
And sustain me with a willing spirit.

PSALM 51:10, 12

20

Why does grace sometimes make me uncomfortable?

I recently had a conversation about grace with a woman. I started by saying that true followers of Jesus were forgiven for *everything*.

"You mean *all* sins?" she said.

"Yes."

"No matter what?"

"Yes."

She thought for a moment. "A Christian becomes an alcoholic?"

"Forgiven."

"Steals from a charity?"

"Yes."

"Gets a casual divorce…then remarries?"

"Yes."

"Deceives a minister."

"Of course."

Her voice tightened; her lips curled. "Pornographer? Homosexual abortionist? Pedophile?"

"Forgiven."

She narrowed her eyes. "And what if the same person did all those things?"

"Yep."

She huffed and stormed away.

One dictionary defines grace as "unmerited favor." A popular Bible dictionary defines it as "favor, kindness, friendship, forgiving mercy."

Sounds nice. So why is it that some of us get antsy about grace?

I've faced three objections. You may have some of your own.

1. Grace gone too far. The woman above wouldn't have been angry with a *little* grace. She just didn't like the idea of *so much* grace. Besides being unfair (see below), too much grace seemed risky to her. She feared it would encourage sin.

Hers seems like a reasonable argument.

2. *Too good to be true.* Some of us can't imagine how anyone—even Christ—would want to offer mercy without conditions. There's got to be a hitch.

Okay, not bad.

3. *Just not fair.* Some people work pretty hard at getting life right. Why should some loser get a clean slate?

Hard to argue with that one.

All these discomforts make sense. The whole notion of boundless, unqualified, unreserved grace for Jesus's little flock breaks every rule of nature I know: "Give an inch, they'll take a mile." "Nuthin's for nuthin'." "A man reaps what he sows."

But what if we take a *non*natural look?

1. Grace Gone Too Far

Well, biblically speaking, exactly how far *should* it go? Paul tells us in Romans 5:20 that "where sin increased, grace abounded all the more." In Ephesians 1:7–8 we read that we are forgiven according to "the riches of His grace which He *lavished* on us."

I'm not seeing limits here.

But what about encouraging sin?

Paul was criticized for that very thing. But he didn't answer by shrinking grace. Instead, he expressed outrage at its abuse. "What shall we say then? Are we to continue in sin so that grace may increase? *May it never be!*" (Romans 6:1–2). Surely, a remorseless Christian better take another look at herself.

So how is grace abuse restrained?

Grace—properly understood—inspires gratitude. "For all things are for your sakes, *so that the grace which is spreading to more and more people may cause the giving of thanks* to abound to the glory of God" (2 Corinthians 4:15). Understanding the depth of our sin and the boundlessness of grace enables a life of obedience through the power of gratitude.

2. Too Good to Be True

> For the word of the cross is foolishness to those who are perishing, but to us who are being saved it is the power of God. (1 Corinthians 1:18)

Enough said.

3. Just Not Fair

Jesus dealt with this complaint in a parable in Matthew 20, where all the workers were paid the same regardless of how many hours they'd worked. It's true: mercy isn't fair. That's why it's called mercy.

Yes, grace really is unnatural...because it's supernatural.

However, in its unlimited, unfathomable, unmerited glory, grace is often not good news to control types, cynics, or the self-righteous. It doesn't affirm their worldviews.

But to the weak, the desperate, and the broken, grace is more than amazing. It's the astonishing gift of immeasurable love.

If we're uncomfortable with lavish grace, we might want to pause and consider why that is. It just may be that we're missing out on the really good part of the good news!

Food for Thought

How far do I think grace should go?

On what basis should it be limited?

Do I resent the forgiveness of the "undeserving"?

Do I think I'm deserving?

Has grace ever seemed amazing in my life?

A PRAYER

O thou mercy of God,
From how abundant a sweetness,…flowest
thou forth unto us!
O boundless goodness of God,
How ought we sinners to be moved by love
of thee!…
O immeasurable goodness,… let that
mercy be shed upon me,
Which proceedeth from the great riches of
that goodness!

SAINT ANSELM OF CANTERBURY (1033–1109),
FROM *DEVOTIONS*

21

Why do I care so much about my reputation?

For some reason that escapes me now, I accepted an invitation to a country club golf outing sponsored by a group of businessmen. Having *never* golfed before, I went searching for my party in a building called the pro shop, sporting my red high-top sneakers.

When I entered, I suddenly noticed no one else in the shop was wearing sneakers.

Or shorts.

And everybody else had shirts with collars.

I found the host and his fellow members, who moved quickly toward a distant corner, shaking their heads, and leaving me abandoned in the middle of the shop with my hands in my pockets. I felt eyes from here and there, but I smiled bravely.

I heard someone call my name from outside. "Let's go, Baker."

"Hang on," I said. I strolled to the counter.

"Yes sir, how can I help you?" The clerk slanted his eyes at the others.

"Well, I think I need my ball," I answered.

The clerk stared.

"My ball... I need my ball."

"I don't get it."

I heard a distant groan. Then someone hurried to my side and hissed, "This isn't miniature golf, you numskull."

Oops.

Few of us like embarrassing ourselves. And our reputations as good, normal people *are* important. Even Paul cared about his. In 2 Corinthians 11 and 12 he goes to great lengths to justify his leadership. He boasted about his reputation *in order to serve them better.*

But I doubt that's why I care about what others think of me. I'm afraid I seek a fine reputation in order to serve *myself.* So I find myself needing a reputation as a wise consultant, amazing writer, or profound teacher. I want to be known, honored, respected, thought well of.

But if I achieve one of these reputations, I quickly feel the need to protect it at all costs. I will soon fear risking it by standing up *to* someone or by standing up *for* someone. I won't dare be honest, lest I be found out.

And that's when I stop being real and become an image.

My reputation becomes an idol—eventually demanding my submission. Enslaved to our reputations, many of us do all sorts of things. We may spend money we don't have, we may gossip, lie, exaggerate, or deceive. The fact is, many fear their reputation more than their conscience.

Regardless of the many forms that reputation idolatry takes, it always leads to bondage.

That's because at the root of reputation idolatry is the most menacing temptation of all—the temptation to look past God's unmerited approval in favor of the approval of others. Ironically, the worst expression of this poor substitute is spiritual obsession. Wanting to be Christlike *so that* others will value our spiritual reputation, we strive endlessly to be affirmed by church communities or pastors. But our work is never enough. So we throw ourselves into more and more ministry, ever more careful to never share the demons that tempt us. We cover ourselves with clean clothes and a smile. And no one will ever know.

Achieving such a "righteous reputation" can eventually morph us into joyless, obsessive, religious fanatics bound up in ourselves, blind to the fact that striving to be Christlike *for the sake of ourselves* is the very opposite of Christlikeness.

In contrast, the Bible offers us the hard but liberating truth: "For all have sinned and fall short of the glory of God" (Romans 3:23).

That's our real reputation.

But that's *not* the end of the story.

Jesus's reputation is stellar—and I am in him! (See 2 Corinthians 5:17.)

And that changes everything.

Being in Christ means I am given *his* reputation. I can be honest in my world. I can show others the dirt under my nails and tell them my secrets. After all, I am covered by the reputation of Jesus…and that's the only one worth caring about.

Food for Thought

How many ways does my concern for reputation determine my actions?

Do I see reputation idolatry in others?

What's the difference between reputation idolatry and trying to be a good witness?

How can I be more aware of Jesus in me?

What difference does it make in my life to be free from reputation idolatry?

A PRAYER

All who see me sneer at me....
They wag the head....
Yet You are He who brought me
forth from the womb;...
I will tell of Your name to my
brethren;...
They will come and will declare
[Your] righteousness.

PSALM 22:7, 9, 22, 31

22

Why don't I know
what I want in life?

A successful entrepreneurial type in my town excelled in everything he did. He was an outstanding businessman with a PhD in history, an accomplished racquetball player, a world-class photographer, a published author, a recorded musician, a certified diver, and had very nearly qualified as a PGA golfer.

He hopped from one interest to the next, always trying something new. I was impressed with his wide range of skills, I respected (and envied) his diverse abilities. His horizon seemed infinite.

So I asked him one day why he chose to do so many things.

He answered, "I just don't know what I want."

I remember those closing months of high school, when I had to make a decision about what to study in college. "So what do you want to be?" was the counselor's question. I had no idea!

Most of us don't know what we want to be in life...or what we want to have, or not have, what we want to do, or where we want to go… We just don't know what we want.

Is that so bad?

I don't know. Maybe not. A certain amount of vagueness in our desires stimulates curiosity, and that can be a good thing. After all, curiosity is a God-given urge to explore, to engage the imagination, to wonder.

But sometimes not knowing what I want reveals a lack of clarity in my life. It's a condition that always seems to disqualify what *is* in favor of what *could be.* So I react to everything around me with a "what if" or a "yeah, but." I bounce from one place to the next, from job to job, hobby to hobby. I get lost.

My vision is blurred because I'm not really sure what I'm looking for. And I've lost sight of what I'm looking for because I've forgotten who I am.

When a grandmother asks her granddaughter, "What do you want to be when you grow up?" she's asking a helpful question. But maybe the deeper question is, "*Who* do you want to be?"

Our wants are ultimately tied to our identities.

Someone who thinks of herself as a stunning beauty will *want* the clothes, the hair, the friends, and the stage that lets her be who she thinks she is. Someone who thinks of herself as a super-Christian will *want* the books, the CDs, the social network, the church, and the affirmation that she thinks supports that. Someone who's not sure who she is will lurch from one set of wants to another.

If we better know who we are, we'll better know what we want.

So the real question becomes: who are we?

King David answered famously in his Twenty-third Psalm: "The LORD is my shepherd, I shall not want." Knowing who he was as a sheep in the Good Shepherd's sheepfold freed him from any concern about having/doing/being anything other than what that meant.

Our identity as Christians is that of followers of Jesus. And so Jesus tells us to not be dissatisfied, worried, or unsettled about things we think we want, but instead to seek his kingdom (see Matthew 6).

Why? Because accepting our identity as kingdom dwellers allows us the freedom to abandon the wants of Self dwellers.

The problem is, accepting that identity is not always easy. Some of us try to cling to identities that are independent of Jesus.

So we live like schizophrenics.

Not good.

So what do we do?

Maybe we need to realize that the issue driving a confusion about our desires is really our struggle for identity.

Life doesn't have to be this way. Asking Jesus to regularly remind us of *who* we are will begin to settle our wants.

And maybe that's the start of realizing that all we really want is to delight in him as he does in us.

Food for Thought

What is it that I want?

Why do I want that?

What does that say about who I am?

How do I "actualize" my identity as a follower?

Do I want what Christ wants?

A PRAYER

When we disclose our wants in prayer,
May we our wills resign;
And not a thought our bosoms share
That is not wholly thine.

JOSEPH D. CARLYLE (1759–1804),
FROM "LORD, WHEN WE BEND
BEFORE THY THRONE"

23

Why are some Christians so hard for me to like?

While vacationing on North Carolina's Outer Banks with friends, I took a walk along the beach in search of solitude. I avoided eye contact with a sand-sitter, only to have him call me over. "Hey, buddy," he shouted.

I groaned inwardly and turned around.

He released a puff of smoke from his cigarette. "I'm Billy," he said in a thick southern accent.

I nodded. "I'm David."

He shook my hand, then proceeded to tell me about nerve damage in his legs, his unemployment, his recent escape from crack cocaine—and his joy in finding Jesus. And when he said, "Jesus," for the second time in his long drawl, his smile spread as wide as the blue horizon.

It didn't take long for me to like Billy.

The next day, one of my friends asked if I'd met Billy on the beach.

I nodded.

"He gave me his entire testimony," my friend said tersely.

I felt my stomach twitch. "And?"

"I told him if he was going to talk about Jesus he had better put that cigarette out!" He folded his arms; he had defended righteousness.

I exploded. I flew into a counter-self-righteous rage and condemned my surprised friend with all the indignity I accused him of heaping on Billy.

But not long after my successful tit for his tat, I started to realize what I had done. It's no wonder we Christians can be hard to like!

I'm afraid those of us who call ourselves Christians make lots of mistakes in the way we treat others and one another. We make it hard for them to find us approachable, trustworthy, or even likable.

I know *I* do.

The fact is, I know more than a few Christians who manage to annoy, anger, and frustrate Christians and non-Christians alike with their "witness."

But just in case this was all in my imagination, I decided to survey some folks and ask them to describe Christians they know. Here are some of the words I heard:

- hypocritical
- judgmental
- critical
- holier-than-thou
- self-righteous
- uptight

- miserable
- pushy
- mean
- demanding

Then I asked if they were talking about me, and they smiled.

Of course, Jesus tells us in Matthew 10:22: "You will be hated by all because of My name." Maybe that's why so many churchgoers don't mind repulsing others—they see it as a sign of faithfulness.

Unfortunately, I'm afraid that some of us are deservedly disliked and for reasons that have nothing to do with Jesus's name's sake. We should pay attention to that; there are many who have abandoned or avoided the faith because of the way some of us have treated them.

The book of Titus has something interesting to say about all this. After two chapters describing the good fruit of sound teaching, the writer concluded: "Do not let anyone despise you" (2:15, NIV).

Yet Jesus had already said we would be hated. So what's going on?

I wonder if we're often despised for the wrong reasons.

I wonder if we've abandoned sound teaching and are bearing witness to some brand of Christianity instead of the gospel? Are we being despised on account of dogmas and lingo and adherance to religious subcultures instead of Christ?

Pay attention to this: the Bible has given us a good test to determine our true loyalties—the good old fruit of the Spirit. If the fruit is what characterizes our lives (instead of that list above) and we're despised, we can be pretty sure it's on account of Jesus. But if we're despised because of the presence of something on that list, we can be pretty sure it's because we're in the wrong.

Food for Thought

How do I describe other Christians?
What is it about their beliefs that contribute to their behaviors?
Am I any different?
What is it about my beliefs that I should examine?
Who or what am I really following?

A PRAYER

O Lord, where you are, shall we then be
To behold you face to face,
And, changed by glorifying grace,
May we resemble who we see yet even now.

ADAPTED FROM "FELLOW TRAVELLERS ON
HEAVEN'S HIGHWAY," JAMES MONTGOMERY
(1771–1854)

24

Why do I have such a complaining spirit?

Picture opens on the scene:

Wife slams oven door. "I don't care about the traffic or what kind of day you had. You're always late for dinner."

Husband clenches fists. "Yeah? Well, why should I rush home for dried-out steak?"

Daughter rolls eyes.

Dad scowls at her. "What do you have to say about it? All you do is watch TV."

Daughter crosses arms. "Don't yell at me because you're a jerk!"

Wife shakes head. "Why are you always so critical of her?"

Husband spins around. "Must have learned it from your mother."

Daughter snickers.

Mother furrows brows.

Husband plops on kitchen chair. "Can we eat? My dry steak's getting cold."

Yikes.

I hope my table talk is never like that…though I can certainly be a world-class complainer.

A few months ago, my wife and I bought a car. *After* the deal was done, I started grumbling about paying too much, about the lousy trade-in value, the unexpected wind noise, and the salesman. I really should have complained about my poor negotiating skills.

Complaining is what I do; it's what lots of us do. Occasionally it's appropriate, but a complaining *spirit* isn't.

So why do some of us have complaining spirits?

The answer is painfully simple: we're constantly dissatisfied with life.

We expect others (and ourselves) to do, say, be, give, have, want, and accomplish the things *we* demand. And they never can. So we're dissatisfied customers of everyone, including ourselves.

The truth is, the Self is never satisfied. So when it's given free reign, it defaults to criticism, self-righteous demands, impossible expectations…and all the many complaints that logically follow.

The problem is that the stakes may be higher than we realize. A complaining spirit is destructive.

Why?

Complaining is usually a form of accusation.

Take a look at every complaint in the little dialogue that opened this chapter. Each is an accusation of one sort or another:

"Late for supper" = "I'm not important to you."

"Dry steak" = "You don't care about me."

"You're always in a bad mood" = "You're selfish."

"Watching too much TV" = "You're a loser."

If you doubt complaints are accusations, think of a time when someone complained about you and ask yourself how it made you feel. Did you feel accused?

The next time you hear yourself complaining, ask what accusations you're making. And remember that the ultimate accuser is Satan (see Revelation 12). He works hard keeping the world complaining because it makes it easy to sustain judgmental spirits and critical natures. He wants us to condemn and feel condemned—the ultimate opposite of feeling loved.

Ponder that a little today.

Now, if all things were as they should be, we'd be satisfied with whatever God is doing in our lives. We'd be searching for compliments, not complaints. We'd be blessing others, not accusing them. But things aren't even close to what they should be. So it really is hard to avoid a complaining spirit.

But there is good news for complainers: God doesn't complain about us, because he doesn't accuse us!

He has no reason to accuse because he is utterly, totally, 100 percent satisfied with us. And that's not because of anything we've done or can do but *because we are in Christ.* God looks at us and sees his son. And Jesus is the son with whom God is well-pleased.

Whatever is worth complaining about has been taken care of at the Cross.

Food for Thought

When I think "complainer," who comes to mind?
Do I have a complaining/accusing spirit?
What does it feel like when someone complains about what
     I do, say, look like, or think?
When has my complaint caused hurt to another?
When has another's complaint hurt me?

A PRAYER

*Grant, Almighty God,…that we may
     obediently follow
whatever he [thy Son] prescribes for us,…
being content with that simplicity
which we have learnt from his Gospel…
     Amen.*

JOHN CALVIN (1509–1564), FROM
COMMENTARY ON EZEKIEL, VOLUME 1

25

Why am I so desperate to be understood?

Mario was a man I knew who liked to stare at walls and put his savings into nickels, insisting that "the dollar may lose value, but a nickel is always worth five cents."

Don't ask me to explain.

His wife, Carmella, was always stressed out. But no one tried to understand her either. We figured it was about the walls and nickels.

They both sought companionship with others. They were desperate to be understood. Mario tried hard to explain his nickels—but most hurried away. Carmella complained of shoulder pains, but no one really listened.

One day the newspaper reported that Mario was arrested for beating his wife with sand-filled socks. Her bruises had never showed...on the outside.

And then we learned that Mario had spent his childhood chained to a basement bed. It was there that his father shoved nickels under the door as a reward for his silence…a silence he could only maintain by staring at the walls.

That's when people finally began to understand.

One of the dictionary definitions of understanding is "sympathetic awareness." That's what Mario and Carmella desperately wanted—and needed. As do lots of us.

When no one hears our cries, when no one feels our pain, sees our situation, or can speak our story back to us, we get anxious. And then our loneliness feels all the worse.

We want to be understood so that we don't feel alone.

That's natural. We weren't created to be alone. Being understood is a connection to somebody. It makes us feel more normal.

Our need to be understood is necessary because we live in a world of relationships.

In our hyperindividualistic world we easily lose sight of the fact that we are designed as relational creatures. Everything about us is organized in terms of someone else: I am somebody's husband, somebody's father, somebody's son, somebody's neighbor, somebody's friend… It's a long list of relationships that are part of our identities.

Being understood within those contexts helps us relate with others more meaningfully. We feel more sane when others "get" us. And when no one understands our reactions, fears, or points of view, we start feeling isolated, maybe even insane.

The good news is that whether others understand us or not, we are already understood by God.

Psalm 103:14 tells us: "For He Himself knows our frame; He is mindful that we are but dust." God understands. He knows all about us—our weaknesses, our gifts, our secret sufferings, our hopes, our disappointments.

But what about a *desperate* need for understanding?

It's helpful to remember that desperation is a symptom. Desperation may be a symptom of truly desperate circumstances, like Mario's and Carmella's. Or it may be a symptom of deep fear; we want to be understood because we're desperately afraid of how we'd ever live without it. Or it may be a symptom of an inflated self; we desperately want to be the center of the world's attention.

So if we are feeling *desperate* for others to understand us, we might just want to pause. We ought not to judge ourselves too quickly, but neither should we ignore the motives of our hearts. The *reason* we're desperate for understanding may be the key to unlocking what it is we really want from others.

Have we forgotten that we are already understood by the One who knows us in our most inward places?

We might just want to turn to the Spirit and ask.

Food for Thought

Am I ever desperate to be understood?
What is it that I most want others to be understanding about?
How does it feel to be understood by someone?
How many people in my life really understand me?
Do I offer sympathetic awareness to others?

A PRAYER

O LORD, You have searched me and
    known me.
You know when I sit down and when
    I rise up;
You understand my thought from afar....
Search me, O God, and know my heart;
Try me and know my anxious thoughts....
And lead me in the everlasting way.

PSALM 139:1-2, 23-24

26

Why do regrets have so much power in my life?

Pete was a really good friend to a young man who lived in a dangerous neighborhood and was hated by many. The young man reminded Pete that the streets would hold the friendship against him. But Pete said it didn't matter. He'd stay loyal at all costs.

One night Pete was eating out with his young friend and a few others, who were talking about the young man's problems. Suddenly Pete had had enough. He stood up and pounded his chest, boasting quite dramatically that he'd stick with his young friend even if someone tried to kill him for it.

Soon after, the young man got threatened. Pete stood up for him at first, but when the chips were down, he turned his back out of fear for his own life. No sooner had he done that when he realized how much of a big-mouth coward he was. He hid in a corner and cried bitterly. Regret became a great weight on his life.

How heavy regrets can be. This is the story of the disciple Peter. I often wonder how much Peter suffered between that awful moment of betrayal and his eventual encounter with the risen Jesus. Imagine, a disciple denying Christ.

It also occurs to me that *I'm* a disciple of Jesus and, like Peter, I deny him on a regular basis. I don't actually say out loud that I'm not a follower of Jesus—but I haven't had a gun to my head lately, so who knows? Still, I deny him in other ways, like avoiding the subject of him altogether or by serving my self.

And so I have regrets. I look back at all the ways I could have been a better father, husband, friend… I wonder how much better life could have been for everyone had I not done this or had done that.

Regrets—they weigh heavy on my soul.

Why?

Regrets have power because I let them.

Many of us let regrets dictate our joy. We let them accuse us. They become sources of discouragement and depression. They turn our eyes to looking back, and they fill our minds with "if only."

Some of us allow regrets to define us… The man who files for bankruptcy says, "I *am* a bad money manager." The woman whose child uses drugs cries, "I *am* a bad mother." And on and on.

Why do we give them so much power?

Sometimes wallowing in regret is easier than the humbling act of receiving forgiveness. That's too bad.

Sometimes we empower regrets because we've lost sight of the fact that God is sovereign over all our failures and is busy turning our failures into good (see Romans 8:28).

The truth is, the weight of regret is unnecessary.

After the Resurrection, Peter met Jesus along the Sea of Galilee, where Jesus asked him three times (the same number of times Peter had denied Jesus) if Peter loved him. Each time that Peter answered yes, he experienced Jesus's forgiveness (see John 21). Did Peter still have regrets for what he did? Probably. But did his regrets have any power over him?

Not after that.

His regrets were absorbed within the sovereignty of God's purposes. Peter learned from them and went on to build the Church.

Regrets are rendered impotent by God's grace.

So maybe we should rethink our regrets.

It's good that we are sad about past mistakes—such sadness helps us remember how much it is that Jesus forgives. But we need to remember that Jesus was never surprised by our failures in the first place. He has *already* redeemed them for his purposes.

Our job is to let them go.

Food for Thought

Can I name my top five regrets?
How much power do they have in my life?
What does that power look like?
Why do I hang on to the regrets I have?
What would life feel like without them?

A PRAYER

But hush, my soul, and vain regrets, be
  stilled;
Find rest in him who is the complement...
Of baffled hope and unfulfilled intent;
In the clear vision and aspect of whom
All longings and all hopes shall be fulfilled.

ARCHBISHOP RICHARD CHENEVIX TRENCH
(1807-1886), FROM "RETURNING HOME"

27

Why do I feel like
such a hypocrite?

A certain minister preached passionately for family values and was
vocal in his opposition to homosexuality. But his congregation was
shocked when he was eventually outed for his homosexual trysts.
When he openly confessed his weaknesses and sought help from
Christian leaders, one of them passed him along for someone else to
help.

Another minister, famous for his tirades against the immorality of
American culture, railed against adultery, fornication, and perversion.
He hung his head when he was caught with a young girl, angrily blam-
ing others, and quickly fleeing the spotlight.

Hypocrisy is an ugly thing. The word stings with accusatory power.

Hypocrisy disappoints; it discredits; it disgusts.

When we spot hypocrisy in another, we may feel suddenly superior. But underneath, some of us have a nagging suspicion that we're
hypocrites too. And when *we* get outed we react in all kinds of crazy

ways. We set up defenses, we pass the buck, we explain, we rationalize, we run.

The *h* word makes things happen.

But what is hypocrisy?

The dictionary defines *hypocrisy* as claiming beliefs that do not conform to behaviors. That seems plain enough. In the stories above, each pastor preached one thing and lived another. By that definition both were hypocrites.

Unfortunately, I know that in my life I regularly claim to believe one thing and act the opposite: I say I trust God, but I worry; I say "God will provide," but I hoard; I say I love others, but I don't help them. I have done things that are diametrically opposed to what I claim to believe. The fact is, I *am* a hypocrite.

It doesn't feel very good to admit that.

And it doesn't make it any better to recognize that any time a Christian sins, she or he is a hypocrite as well. That sad fact certainly doesn't let any of us off the hook. But it does change the conversation a little. The real issue may not be whether we are hypocrites or not—because all of us are.

What matters is whether we care or not.

In the story above, the first minister was shocked by his own hypocrisy, confessed, and asked for help. He saw his hypocrisy and became a *struggling hypocrite.*

Strugglers fight against their inconsistencies because they've accepted their sin. They care about making things right.

The second pastor never intended for his behaviors to line up with his teaching. He never cared. The only thing he struggled with was not getting caught. He was a *rebellious hypocrite*. His is a very different picture.

But there's a third kind of hypocrite, like the Levite who crossed the street to avoid the Samaritan. Perhaps unaware of their own inconsistencies, these are the *blind hypocrites*.

It's important to consider what kind of hypocrite we are. If we're blind, we need to listen more carefully. If we're rebellious, we need to face the ugliness of our ways. But if we are struggling, we can be thankful that the Spirit has opened our eyes to see the painful truth of ourselves.

Seeing ourselves as we are is always a blessing.

It means we are more aware of our sin. And that helps us better see the greatness of Jesus's love. As odd as it sounds, strugglers may actually want to ask the Spirit to reveal more hypocrisy in their lives! When strugglers admit their hypocrisy they are ready to receive Christ's love. It's then, in a state of grace, that they are enabled and motivated to take a few more baby steps toward more consistent living.

Food for Thought

Do I ever feel like a hypocrite?

What makes me feel most like one?

How does it feel to be called a hypocrite?

Have I spotted hypocrisy in others? It is any different than my own?

Am I able to admit my hypocrisy?

A PRAYER

Let thy goodness, like a fetter,
Bind my wandering heart to thee.
Prone to wander, Lord, I feel it,
Prone to leave the God I love;
Here's my heart, O take and seal it,
Seal it for thy courts above.

ROBERT ROBINSON (1735–1790),
FROM "COME, THOU FOUNT
OF EVERY BLESSING"

28

Why do I try so hard to fit in?

When I was a little boy, my aunt threw a birthday party for my six-year-old cousin. Among the dozen or so kids was five-year-old Esther, who had just moved in next door. She tried to join in but was pretty much ignored. So she found a corner and stared at her ice cream.

Eventually my aunt decided that we should play a game. She put us in a circle and offered a prize to whoever could make the best animal imitation. Someone did a chicken, another did a dog, one a cat, and so it went around the circle with everyone actually doing pretty well.

Until poor Esther.

She really blew it with a terrible pig squeal.

Well, the kids snorted and pointed fingers until my aunt stepped in. She wrapped her arm around Esther's shoulders.

The next to go was a little boy who looked kindly at Esther before deliberately delivering the worst donkey bray ever. Now the circle turned on him…mocking and jeering without mercy.

Among the scorners was Esther.

She had found a way to fit in.

If you ever doubted the human urge to be accepted by a group, just watch the fans at a sporting event. They wear the colors, cheer the same, boo together, and high-five perfect strangers. It's not necessarily a bad thing, but it can all seem rather tribal.

Maybe it *is* tribal. The urge to *belong* is driven by the basic human need to have relationship. Since all of us are created in God's relational image (the Trinity), relationship is not optional. Sanity demands that we associate with others. Fitting in is important because it's not good for us to be alone (see Genesis 2:18).

We want to fit in because we are hard-wired to belong.

Belonging feels good. And so in our deep need to belong, we find all sorts of ways to join a group and then seek ways to stay in it. Sometimes we join around a hobby, sometimes a church or a small group within the church, and sometimes it's family. Of course, the extent of our interest is impacted by our individual design. Extroverts are more likely to crave belonging than introverts—but *all* of us need others.

Sometimes, however, we suddenly realize that something's wrong. In our need to fit in, we find ourselves abandoning someone who's been disapproved by others or we choose silence over confrontation.

When belonging becomes more important than doing what's right, we should ask ourselves why it has such power.

The truth is, we may be longing for the *wrong things*.

One test is to consider how we feel if we imagine ourselves out of the group. Scared? Alone? Devalued?

And we may be seeking to belong in the *wrong places.*

Another test is to consider the rules of conformity. If a place of belonging *demands* conformity, it's probably an unhealthy place to be.

If we search our hearts, we may find that we have *unhealthy* associations because we've simply lost sight of where we really belong: in and to Jesus. That's why he invites us to take communion. It's a tangible reminder that *"He who eats My flesh and drinks My blood abides in Me, and I in him"* (John 6:56).

In him we never need to be scared, feel alone, or feel devalued. And he does not demand blind conformity in order to fit in with him.

Belonging to Jesus means we already fit into his kingdom.

And his kingdom is a place of belonging where we are accepted, unconditionally. Focusing more intentionally on our belonging in Christ sets us free to speak up, to defend the weak, to think deeply, and to challenge others. We are free because no matter what happens, we still have a place to belong...*always.* Paul reminds us in Romans 8 that nothing—*nothing*—can separate us from the love of Christ.

Now that's the kind of "fitting in" that feels really good.

Food for Thought

Is "fitting in" a theme in my life?

Where or to whom do I want to belong? Why?

Have I made others feel that they didn't fit in?

Why does belonging to Christ not always feel like enough?

How might I be more aware of my belonging to him?

A PRAYER

'Tis only in thee hiding
I feel my life secure;
Only in thee abiding,
The conflict can endure.

JAMES G. DECK (1802–1884),
FROM "O LAMB OF GOD,
STILL KEEP ME"

29

Why am I so dependent on order in my life?

It was a lovely summer Friday evening when my wife and I headed for the movies. As we approached the door, I reached for my cell phone to turn it off, when it rang. To my surprise a neighbor was calling. "Your steers are loose and they just crossed the creek."

I felt a rush of anxiety. "All of them?"

"Looks like it."

I sped home, and my wife and I ran down the valley through thorny fence rows, stinging nettles, and scratchy cornfields until well past dark. No luck.

The next morning we got up before dawn and eventually found the little herd about a half mile away. After an exhausting couple of hours of running, hooting, and flanking maneuvers, we finally got them home.

Frustrated, I plopped on a chair. I learned that a visiting relative had left a gate open! I guzzled some iced tea and stared out the window.

Grrrrr.

Most of us crave order in our lives. It's what we think keeps things under control—*our* control mostly. And sure enough, whenever we lose control, *dis*order shows up. At first glance you might think that's what had me stewing.

But that was only part of it.

I had been reminded that I can't control my life.

The truth is, there's always a relative lurking around the corner.

But sometimes it's far worse than that: the boss hands us a pink slip; the doctor looks away as he pronounces the *c* word; the call from the police comes in the middle of the night.

We're right to keep our lives tidy—"all things must be done properly and in an orderly manner" (1 Corinthians 14:40). But living lives of *order dependence* is different; it's an addiction that ultimately controls *us*. It's something to look out for.

Order dependence is really a form of idolatry.

From it we seek security, confidence, well-being, affirmation, peace.

Like all idols, however, addictions eventually destroy us…

…because they lie.

Order addiction tells us we can control what we can't. Try as we may, the world keeps opening our gates. In response, anger and fear take hold; anxiety is just a frustration away.

The truth is that no addiction ever keeps its promise. And order dependence can finally swallow us up into the dark prison of perfectionism where every relationship we have is likely to be destroyed.

The only source of order is God, and he keeps order in ways that are not usually what we expect. Sometimes *he* opens our gates! Ask Job.

"In whirlwind and storm is His way," said Nahum (1:3). If you think about it, Jesus spent much of his life *disrupting* lives...before setting them in order *his way*. "I came to set a man against his father, and a daughter against her mother" (Matthew 10:35).

Order is not true order unless it's God's order.

When our gates are left open, we'll surely be frustrated. That's natural. But we need to eventually come to our senses and remember that everything that is, is within the order of God's mysterious sovereignty.

Therefore, what looks like chaos never is.

In the end, God is working out all things for good (see Romans 8:28). This God of whirlwinds and disruption whom we follow will ultimately prove himself to be "not a God of disorder but of peace" (1 Corinthians 14:33, NIV). And that's a comfort.

Now, if we find that truth to be elusive in our lives, we might want to ask ourselves *why*? What is driving our order dependence? Insecurity? Pride?

What's keeping *me* from trusting the whirlwind?

The answers are important.

Food for Thought

Am I addicted to order? Why?

How does life feel when it turns chaotic?

Do I impose my ideas of order on others?

Does perfectionism characterize my life?

Where do I think God is when life gets turned upside down?

A PRAYER

When my world is unsettled,
Please come.
When my world is undone,
Please come.
When all seems lost to chaos and storm,
Please come
And show me that I am still in the hollow of your hand.

30

Why don't I feel safe at church?

Before Robyn's divorce she told me about her new church. "You should visit," she said.

"What's it like?" I asked.

"The minister really knows his Bible," she said.

"That's nice. Is he helping you with your marriage stuff?"

"Well, he tells me exactly what to do."

"And what's that?"

"To do better."

"Oh," I said. "What do you think about that?"

"Why should that matter?"

"I just thought…"

"At least he has answers."

"Good ones?"

"Right ones. And he holds me accountable."

"To what?"

"To doing what's right."

"Oh," I said. "So you're happy there."

"Yeah. And the pastor's very pleased I've brought guests."

"Oh yeah? What do they think?"

"They said I should have warned them."

After a tough divorce, Robyn's view of her church changed. She received scolding letters from some and was shunned by others. She became depressed, obsessively self-critical, untrusting, and dangerously despondent, until she finally fled the church in shame. "It just doesn't feel safe there anymore," she finally admitted.

She wonders if the stress has contributed to her recent cancer.

Was Robyn's church really unsafe?

Robyn had been drawn to a church she thought of as devout and confident. Fair enough. But she described a church that was controlling, performance oriented, and obsessed with conformity. Her story reminds me of one of my own family members who had skipped church for a few weeks only to find an elder peering in her window on a Sunday morning.

Are these the qualities of a safe church?

Now, I doubt that most "unsafe" churches think of themselves as such. The problem is, C. S. Lewis, writing in *God in the Dock: Essays on Theology and Ethics,* observed, "Those who torment us for our own good will torment us without end for they do so with the approval of their own conscience."

What some churches may sincerely believe to be right and good just might not be.

The sad truth is, if a church doesn't feel safe, it likely isn't.

Notice I didn't say "comfortable." Churches may (should) not always feel comfortable—but churches should always be safe. Why?

Because, according to Romans 12, in the face of a broken world, churches are called to be safe houses devoted to love, rejoicing in hope, contributing to the needs of the saints, practicing hospitality, selfless, prayerful, diligent, persevering in tribulation, weeping with those who weep, humble, peaceful, serving, and good.

That's what a safe church looks like. That's what Jesus looks like.

And like Jesus, his churches are to be safe hospices of care for messy lives.

Churches where people act as if they're above the struggles and the smells, where they deny or marginalize the ugly realities of life and don't get dirty in healing others, are unsafe. Why? *Because they've fixated on what's coming and not what is.*

Imagine shaming a child for her nightmares, telling her to "get over" a broken arm, or beating her for spilled milk. Tragically, that's not very different from what happens in some churches.

As they lose sight of human frailty and the pressures that life brings, they lose sight of grace. And the more we lose sight of grace, the more we demand the impossible "shoulds" of a kingdom not yet perfected. The result: anxiety, repression, denial, suspicion, oppression, and abuse.

Toxic religion.

So how do we know if we're in an unsafe church?

Remember the fruit test? If a church lives the fruit of the Spirit (see Galatians 5), we should take another look at ourselves and not the church. Maybe we're uncomfortable because we should be.

But if we don't see good fruit—if we smell smoke—it's probably time to find a new church to call home…one that really *is* safe—like Jesus.

Food for Thought

Do I now or have I ever felt unsafe at church? Why? When? How did I respond to feeling that way?
Have I made others feel unsafe at church or even in my life?
What makes me feel safe at church, at home, with friends, with God?

A PRAYER

Let all who take refuge in You be glad,
Let them ever sing for joy;
And may You shelter them,
That those who love Your name may
exult in You.

PSALM 5:11

31

Why do I resent authority?

Cindy is a woman who chafes against every source of authority. And who could blame her? Her husband was abusive, going so far as to punch her in the stomach when she was pregnant. She eventually sought relief from the elders of her church, who insisted "those things don't happen here." They reluctantly agreed to talk to the husband but warned Cindy sternly that she needed to submit to him *no matter what*. And unless he cheated on her, she had better not think about divorce because God would punish her for it.

Roy is a young salesman who bristles at the idea of having a manager looking over his shoulder. So he finds ways to be insubordinate without getting fired. And when not working, he spites the rest of the world by tuning out with his iPod. For Roy, freedom means never having to say, "I'll do it your way."

Cindy and Roy have different reasons for resenting authority: Cindy was wounded by oppression; Roy worships self. But they share a common desire: *autonomy.*

Autonomy is the myth of absolute independence.

Like so many of us, Cindy and Roy are tempted in the same way that Adam and Eve were when Satan told them they could be "like God" (Genesis 3:5). Imagining freedom from all authority, even God's, is the most powerful seduction of all.

Independence is a highly valued virtue for many of us. Actually, the desire to be free from oppression is a healthy attitude. Liberty is a powerful theme all through the Bible. Moses led the Hebrews out of captivity; Jesus came to break the bondage of sin and death.

God wants his people to be free. But he doesn't want any of us chasing after the illusion of autonomy.

Why? For starters, it's a rejection of his love. Love gladly submits one's will to another's—like Jesus submitting himself to the cross for our sakes. Imagine if God did not "so love the world" (see John 3:16).

But autonomy wants nothing to do with that kind of love. Instead, it drives our resentment of authority and keeps us in a constant state of rebellion.

However, autonomy is an illusion; it's not real because we are created as *dependent* creatures. Autonomy is not our natural state. It cannot be achieved.

That's why the fight for total independence inevitably leads to stress.

It's exhausting for Cindy to battle the many authorities in her life. It's hard work for Roy to sustain his self-deception. Both are fighting for a lie.

In Romans 6, Paul reminds us that we are either servants of sin or servants of grace. In either case, we do live under the authority of a master—and we cannot serve two of them (see Luke 16:13).

The important question to ask then is, *who* is your master?

Cindy's master is not her husband or her elders. Cindy's master is Christ. But she has walked away from his comfort, guidance, and wisdom because her fear has driven her into herself. Cindy could have stood against the oppression she suffered—at home and at church—by claiming the rights she has been given under the authority of her Savior.

Pride has become Roy's acting master. Worshiping himself instead of Christ is what sin wants him to do, and he is obeying. As a result, he denies himself the joy of living freely under the loving lordship of Christ.

Those of us who struggle with authority might want to pause for a moment and consider whether the lure of autonomy is at work within us. If so, the joy of *true* freedom is just a prayer away. The Spirit is waiting for us, longing to restore us to the liberties of the kingdom!

Food for Thought

How do I react to authority?

How would I have counseled Cindy?

Do I ever look like Roy?

How do I constrain legitimate authorities in my life?

Who/what are they?

What does freedom under God look like?

A PRAYER

Merciful God! Thou who hast redeemed
     [me] from everlasting servitude,
I pray that I might not rebel against Thy
     order,
nor begrudge other people their higher
     station,
but that I might obey Thy will with a
     cheerful heart,
and that I do not regard it otherwise
     than that I were serving Thee.

THE LITTLE TREASURE OF PRAYERS, 1923

32

Why am I so easily disappointed by life?

Robert is a friend of mine. He's a young minister with a wife, two daughters, and a son. He was teaching an adult Sunday school class a couple of years ago when he set his lesson aside and made an announcement:

"My ministry has gone nowhere. This church has let me down; my family lets me down; my friends let me down... It seems like Jesus lets me down every day. I'm not the man I thought I'd be. Nothing makes me happy; nothing makes me sad. I feel dead inside. Life isn't even close to what I expected it to be."

Well, if it weren't for the sniffles of his wife you could have heard a pin drop. But he wasn't through.

"I'm pudgy, I'm bald, and I don't like my kids. I have no more dreams; I've lost hope."

Now *that* is an honest man.

Robert was having a bad day, but he meant every word that he said. And if you or I don't relate to the particulars of his announcement, I'm sure most of us can relate to the spirit of his feelings.

Disappointment is a companion that's hard to shake. It shows up in every relationship, every activity. It's always just around the corner, ready to dash joy.

So where does disappointment come from?

From failed expectations.

Without expectations it'd be impossible to be disappointed. So while it's not possible (or desirable) to have none, it's important to pay attention to them.

Expectations regulate every relationship. They frame the way we see life.

Lots of expectations are perfectly reasonable. And reasonable expectations lead to reasonable disappointments. But if disappointment is *characterizing* our lives, we can be pretty sure that our expectations may be out of line. And that's a problem.

Like Robert, the first thing we may need is an expectation checkup:

- Are we expecting too much?
- Are we expecting the wrong things?
- How do others react to our expectations?

These questions are important because *unreasonable* expectations lead to resentments that will eventually suffocate joy: Unreasonable expectations damage relationships. Unreasonable expectations can make us unreasonable people.

So why do we create unreasonable expectations?

It's probably because we've decided we know what's best; we believe we know how life *should* be, so we try to control our world our way. This requires expecting things from life, and those expectations (soon to become demands) are whispered in our ears by an insatiable little voice...

Pride.

Help is not found in abandoning all expectations. As Christians we should live "expectantly" (Micah 7:7)! It certainly is possible to expect too little, and giving up on life is no way to live. As followers of Jesus we have good reasons to dream big. And while a life of dreams may end with some disappointments, a life without dreams just ends.

So we need to keep dreaming, keep hoping, keep expecting. And we should give ourselves room to feel some disappointment. After all, some expectations are good and some disappointments are appropriate.

Paul made an interesting comment in 1 Corinthians 15:43: "Our bodies now *disappoint* us" (NLT). He said this because he looked forward to a new body in the coming resurrection. However, his disappointment in his present body didn't steal his hope.

Properly placed expectations can inspire us in healthy ways toward what can be, and healthy disappointment can helpfully remind us of how things shouldn't be.

And an important key in all this is realizing that even healthy expectations should be *hopes* and *not demands*. This is important because…

Disappointment loses its destructive powers when expectations are disconnected from demands.

Making demands of life guarantees unhealthy disappointment. But when we stop "leaning on our own understanding" (see Proverbs 3:5), we let go of demands. We become liberated from a worldview based on disappointment.

So how do we let go?

We ask the Spirit to show us our hearts; we ask to be filled with the faith to believe that our disappointments are sometimes invitations to understand hope differently.

For the Christian, optimism—not disappointment—is graciously offered as a way of life. "*Hope does not disappoint,* because the love of God has been poured out within our hearts through the Holy Spirit" (Romans 5:5).

Food for Thought

Does disappointment characterize my life?
What do I expect from life?
Who has let me down? How have I reacted?
What happens when I'm disappointed?
Why do I resist God's sovereignty?

A PRAYER

Open my eyes to see as you see;
Open my heart to expect by faith;
Open my hands to hold hope loosely;
And let my disappointments fade away
    in your love.

33

Why am I bored with church, the Bible, and Jesus?

My grandfather was a preacher. He worked hard on his sermons and spent lots of energy delivering them. That's why I look back sadly at the yawns, the drooping heads, and the window gazers who couldn't have cared less about anything he said. I even remember myself as a nine-year-old boy, tipping over in the front pew and falling sound asleep on the hard oak.

I wonder how he felt knowing that he was boring the people he loved…even his grandson.

Nowadays I sometimes do a little teaching of my own. It's really disappointing to look over an audience to see what my grandfather saw! I wonder what they'd think if I was honest and told them I've sometimes been bored to death preparing their lesson!

I wonder if Grandpop had that problem too.

I'm pretty sure most Christians would admit to being bored with all things Jesus at least some of the time. Frankly, I'm willing to go further and say many of us may be bored with him and with our faith *a lot* of the time.

And why not?

It's easy to get bored with all sorts of things, especially in today's fast-paced culture. If something's not shiny, moving fast, and making lots of noise, we yawn. Yesterday's news might as well be last year's news.

Nothing stays *meaningful* very long.

But what does all this have to do with my Christian life? Shouldn't that be different?

Probably.

But I'm afraid our faith easily loses meaning for some of us. It all can seem so…so irrelevant. We get tired of thinking, hearing, talking, and singing about Jesus and the Bible. So I hear people (and myself) saying, "I just don't care about that right now."

But we really do care about things that *mean* something to us. When we watch a movie or a television show, we're never bored with the ones *that matter* to us.

Things that matter to us don't bore us.

Now, we all know that Jesus *should* matter, but it's sometimes hard to feel that he does.

Until our worlds collapse.

When our child is desperately ill or our marriage is falling apart or we're unemployed or facing death…Jesus suddenly matters a lot. He doesn't bore us then. We become obsessed with prayer, with Scripture, with the church community.

Now, before we all start feeling guilty, let me ask: Is this any different in other categories in our lives? Don't we get bored with our jobs...until they're at risk? Don't we take our spouses for granted... until they suddenly matter more?

My point is that boredom is a human response. Things that really do matter start to bore us when we lose sight of their meaning in our lives. And that's easy to do.

So how do we stay aware of how much Jesus really does matter to us?

I'm really not sure.

But if we care at all, I think a starting place is to *tell him* plainly that he bores us, his church bores us, and so does his Bible.

I wonder how he'll answer.

Will he gather us close and remind us that we belong to him— no matter what?

Will Jesus gently remind us that we are daughters and sons of God, princesses and princes of the King of kings (see Romans 8:16)?

I think that'd be one way for him to remind us of how much he matters in our lives. Being reminded that we are his sisters and brothers—royalty in the service of redeeming the Creation—might surely add meaning to our day.

How could such a vision be boring?

Food for Thought

Am I bored with my faith?

Do I ever get excited when I think about Jesus?

How does it feel to imagine myself as a princess or prince
in the kingdom of God?

What could a fresh vision of who I am mean to my life?

What could an embrace of my identity mean to how
I see Jesus?

A PRAYER

Come, Holy Spirit, heavenly Dove,
With all thy quickening powers;
Kindle a flame of sacred love
In these cold hearts of ours.

ISAAC WATTS (1674–1748), FROM
"COME, HOLY SPIRIT, HEAVENLY DOVE"

34

Why can't I relax around God?

I know a young man—we'll call him Don. He lives at home but works in a clothing shop. He spends his days chattering happily with prospective customers. His supervisor says he's one of the most cheerful, engaging salesmen he's ever seen.

When Don comes home and his father enters the scene, he clams up. His shoulders tense; his jaw tightens; his speech becomes clipped. At dinner his feet tap nervously under the table. He avoids eye contact, and his energy drains away. He fades from conversation and tries to melt into silence.

He reminds me of myself when I imagine God is close by.

I asked some self-described Christians if they felt comfortable around God. Here's a sampling of their answers:

- "If I've kept up with my devotions."
- "Only if I have a clear conscience."
- "Sometimes, but usually only when I'm praying."
- "Are you kidding?"

- "I try not to think about it."
- "No. Never."

Considering we're *always* in God's presence, this is troubling.

Sadly, many of us tense up like Don with his father. If we imagine him next to us, we start to hyperventilate...figuring he's come to correct us, punish us, demand more—to remind us of how disappointed he is.

So what do we do when we can't relax around someone?

We may hide by avoiding eye contact or limiting speech. Or we may try to please and appease; we start working for approval. Or we stop being who we are and become who we think they want us to be.

That's what we do when we think God is near. But maybe the easiest way to relax around God is to forget him entirely.

So what's up?

Somewhere along the way, we got the wrong idea of who God is.

We might want to think about that. Why is it that we are so uneasy? Is he really the critical, demanding, wrathful, ready-to-pounce Judge?

Well, sort of...to his enemies.

But are we his enemy?

No.

So who is he to us? *"Behold, then the...severity of God; to those who fell,...but to you [us!], God's kindness"* (Romans 11:22).

It's good to pay attention to the whole person of God, but it's most important to remind ourselves *every day* who God is...*to us.*

So who is he *to us?*

He is our Father, our Savior, our Comforter.

And *how* is he *to us*?

Here's the short list:

- merciful (see Psalm 145:8)
- compassionate (see Joel 2:13)
- slow to anger (see Psalm 103:8)
- kind (see Titus 3:4)
- patient (see 2 Peter 3:9)
- accepting (see Romans 15:7)
- gracious (see Psalm 111:4)
- forgiving (see Ephesians 4:32)
- loving (see Psalm 86:5)
- safe (see 2 Timothy 4:18)

Like I said, that's the short list.

But if this is true, why is it so hard for us to relax around God?

It may be that we think of God as if he's someone else we know—like an abusive power figure in our lives. Or maybe we simply don't believe that he is who he says he is… And that may be because some church leaders are so consumed with scaring sinners into salvation or keeping saints in line that they only ever talk about "who God is" to his enemies; they forget to remind us that we are his much-loved and well-cared-for children.

It's not easy for limited humans to see and believe in the goodness of God. But we can focus on the many scriptures that teach us that truth. And, like Moses, we can ask of the Lord, "Show me Your glory" (Exodus 33:18).

Try to imagine his goodness suddenly passing in front of you, and see if you don't actually begin to relax.

Food for Thought

How do I feel when I think of God's presence?

If I'm *un*comfortable, why?

If I'm comfortable, why?

Do I try to make myself more comfortable by "doing" things? What are they?

How would relaxing around God make my life different?

A PRAYER

I will extol you, my God;
I will eagerly utter the memory of your
abundant goodness.
For you are gracious and merciful,
slow to anger and great in lovingkindness.
You sustain all who fall
and raise all who are bowed down.
You open your hand.
You are kind in all your deeds;
you keep all who love you safe.
Bless your holy name forever and ever.

ADAPTED FROM PSALM 145

35

Why are my feelings so easily hurt?

I had a great-uncle Levi. Uncle Levi was a kind and gentle farmer with a tender heart. The problem with Uncle Levi was that he needed constant affirmation. Without it he felt rejected—hurt. So he could never take a joke. Of course, he could barely take a compliment, a vague comment, or an inopportune sigh either.

Once a cousin of mine thought he was being nice when he told Uncle Levi that his corn rows (real ones, not his hair) were "pretty straight." Uncle Levi interpreted that as being a lousy planter. Another cousin told him he could sing almost as well as Great-Grandpop. The "almost" was a problem.

I'm still not sure what I was thinking when I sent Uncle Levi a birthday card with a photograph of a wrinkled-up old man on the front. It read, "You're not getting any younger or any better looking. But we love you anyway. Happy 85th."

Bad choice.

Interestingly, Uncle Levi threw all his cards away except that one.

Uncle Levi may be an extreme example, but all of us are hurt by others from time to time. We may feel diminished by a sideways look, a dismissive answer, an unreturned call. It's all to be expected. But when we are too easily hurt, when emotional stings become major dramas in our lives, we've given away too much power.

So why do we do that?

It may be that we're depending on the wrong things to feel "unhurt," that is, accepted, secure, or even loved.

The truth is, what hurts me says a lot about what I need.

Being overly sensitive speaks volumes about what I depend on for emotional well-being. When things I depend on to feel good about myself are not affirmed, *I* feel reduced, ridiculed, and even rejected...and all that is hurtful.

For one young woman I know, a snide remark about an out-of-date handbag really, truly, is wounding. She interprets it as an evaluation of her taste, and to her, good taste reveals social worth.

I know a man who brushes aside insulting remarks about his parenting skills, but a complaint about his money management throws him into a tailspin. He takes it as a judgment on his manhood.

When we find ourselves reeling from hurt, we may want to name those things that we depend on to *not* feel hurt.

Have we relied on good looks, money, reputation, education, or even spiritual growth to feel good about ourselves? Have we become dependent on the approval of friends, family, co-workers, or our pastors? Have we so identified ourselves with things, images, or relationships that we feel really good when they're affirmed and really bad when they're rejected?

Jesus Christ came to destroy the power of contempt, insult, and offense by taking all the rejection the world could muster and hanging it on the cross. He now invites us to look to him *and to nothing else* for approval. He wants us to believe that if God is for us, what does it matter who is against us? (See Romans 8:31.)

Jesus wants to be enough for us so that debilitating hurt is kept at bay.

Of course, if I'm honest I have to admit that he isn't always enough.

I have a long way to go. There are things that people can do or say that hurt me, that feel insulting and demeaning. I need him to expose the many things that I ultimately value more than him. I need his grace to enable me to lean on him alone so that the wounds of the world—though they may sting—will finally lose their power in my life.

Food for Thought

Who or what most hurts my feelings?

Why do I give these things power?

Do others tiptoe around me for fear of hurting my feelings?

How can I be sensitive to others' feelings without enabling unwarranted sensitivity?

Why don't I value Jesus's acceptance more than others'?

A PRAYER

Father, the greatest lesson my soul must
    learn
Is that you alone are enough for its needs.
This is the lesson you want to teach;
And this is the crowning discovery of my
    whole life.
Father, you are enough!

ADAPTED FROM *THE GOD OF ALL COMFORT,*
HANNAH WHITALL SMITH (1832–1911)

36

Why is justice so important to me?

Near my hometown a Christian businessman was cheated by another Christian to the tune of many hundreds of thousands of dollars. Trying to honor Scripture, the victim never took the perpetrator to court and so was never vindicated. But though the victim had followed one mandate of Scripture (to avoid the court when possible), he refused another—to forgive—and lived his remaining years in an unforgiving, depressive rage, embittered with a man and also with a God whom he believed had failed to be just.

It was heartbreaking to watch this man self-destruct. He truly was a victim of injustice, and so I understood his frustration. He had been treated unfairly, even sinfully. After all, he did have his rights.

And God cares about these things.

The Bible identifies all kinds of rights granted to people over the ages: rights to water, rights of widows, of the poor, of marriage. This man's rights had been violated and, worse yet, violated by a fellow Christian.

But he was unable to look beyond the issue of his rights. Unable to forgive, he remained fixated on the Law. As a result, he turned inward and cold, suspicious of others, hardhearted, and self-righteous. He died a miserable man, imprisoned by an obsession with justice.

So what do I want when *I'm* wronged? What happens when *my* rights are violated? How do I react when *my* cheek is slapped?

I get pretty ticked off.

My jaw tightens and I clench my fists. I fantasize about vengeance. I mutter those special four-letter words.

Are any of us really so very different from the man above? Most of us suffer nagging bitterness from old wounds. In fact, I'm quite sure that many of us can name a number of people who "owe" us. We too want things "made right."

Or to be more honest, we want to get even.

Getting even feels so good.

And when we don't get even, many of us become angry, bitter, and vengeful. We scream at other drivers, refuse to speak to neighbors, and slander reputations tit for tat.

Why?

I suspect our pride has us deceived into thinking we deserve to be treated as if we've never mistreated another, and it demands that we get every bit of what we deserve.

Yes, God seeks justice and so should we. He grieves when we are oppressed or taken advantage of, and he demands justice on our behalf. But what we forget is that Jesus already paid the price for others' violations against us…and for our violations against them. We don't need to seek vengeance.

But like the wronged businessman, we fixate on the Law; we lose sight of our own sin, the Cross, and God's gracious love even for those who have sinned against us.

Is obsessing about getting what we deserve the way we really want to live our lives?

Sure, it feels good to demand justice and deliciously good to get it. Yet if we're not careful, this just might leave us in a particularly awkward position with God. Do we really want what we deserve from him?

I doubt it.

The good news is that God does not treat his children according to the demands of justice.

Thanks to the Cross, he treats us with mercy instead.

And mercy, by definition, is not just. Let's thank him for that.

And let's learn from that. How liberated the businessman could have been had he focused his attention on God's mercy in his own life. Dwelling prayerfully on God's grace in his *un*deserving life would have changed the way he treated others.

Recognizing God's forgiveness of his own many "debts" in life would have empowered him to forgive the "debts" owed him by the other (see Matthew 6:12).

Food for Thought

Do I remember times when I've been wronged?
How did I react? Do I still react that way?
Do I remember times when I've wronged another?
How do I respond to mercy and forgiveness? Can I offer either?
What does it feel like to receive mercy from another?

A PRAYER

Our Father who is in heaven,
Hallowed be Your name.
Your kingdom come
Your will be done,
On earth as it is in heaven.
Give us this day our daily bread.
And forgive us our debts, as we also have
*   forgiven our debtors.*
And do not lead us into temptation,
*   but deliver us from evil.*
For Yours is the kingdom and the power
*   and the glory forever. Amen.*

THE LORD'S PRAYER, MATTHEW 6:9–13

37

Why don't I seem
to love myself more?

Sleepily, I took my seat in the airplane and dutifully fastened my seat belt. The flight attendant took her familiar place at the front of the plane and began to do the safety presentation. Since I usually feel guilty for not paying attention, I obediently kept my eyes open and listened to the whole thing.

Typically I'm bored, but on one flight I heard the attendant say something that actually piqued my interest. She looked at a mother with two young children and reminded them that mothers should be sure to put on their own oxygen masks first.

Hmm. I know enough mothers to wonder if that would ever happen. After all, surely their maternal instincts would kick in and they'd be grabbing masks for their children before going for their own. Besides, the whole idea sounded wrong. I've been taught to always put others ahead of myself. But that's when it hit me: How can anyone really take care of others unless they take care of themselves? How can I love others if I don't love myself?

﹡﹡﹡

Many of us probably have attended churches where the love of one-self was discouraged as just plain selfishness. And why not? We see the love of self abused in so many ways all around us, everything from attitudes of entitlement to self-absorbed gluttony.

Nevertheless, Jesus commands us to "love your neighbor *as your-self*" (Matthew 22:39). It's perfectly appropriate, therefore, even necessary, to love ourselves.

But how do we love ourselves without being selfish? On what basis do we put on our own masks first?

Well, what is love, anyway?

The English word for *love* is unfortunately broad, so I like to define love simply as "any act or attitude that points to Christ." After all, Jesus Christ *is* love.

With that in mind, how do I love myself in the way Jesus would want me to? How do I love myself without being selfishly in love with myself?

To state the obvious, it's not by putting my interests above others'. But it's also not by ignoring my own interests, something I'm tempted to do as a "good" Christian. Instead, I think proper love of oneself may be learning to relate to ourselves as God relates to us.

Seeing ourselves as Christ sees us is a way of loving ourselves as Christ loves us.

Sounds easy enough, but I think many of us have trouble with it.

I do, because of my tendency to neglect grace. I just don't get the idea that when Christ sees me, he loves who I am no matter what. Instead, my pride wants me believing that I'm loved by Jesus…according to my performance. And so that's how I love myself.

That's why I'm the one who'll ignore my oxygen mask on the plane.

But I'll eventually suffocate in my own self-righteousness.

The truth is, a healthy love of self does not come from performance.

So where does it come from? First John 4:19 answers: "We love, because He first loved us." This verse is rightly used to remind us of how we are enabled to genuinely love others. But it also tells us that grace is the source of healthy self-love.

Healthy love of self comes from understanding the immensity of grace.

Grace is the oxygen mask we need to love ourselves. That's why it's not selfish to take the mask first. Doing so means we're letting go of our pride and the dangerous temptations of performance love.

But how do we begin to apprehend grace?

We ask the Spirit to fill us with the grace we need to see grace! For grace really is like the airplane oxygen masks: it's hanging right before our very eyes.

All we need to do is take hold…and breathe.

Food for Thought

What does loving myself look like?
Do I love myself?
How do I love myself without loving self?
How does Christ see me?
How does grace help me love?

A PRAYER

O Lord, let my ears hear of grace unbounded,
Let my eyes see your love in my mirror,
Let my lips taste the sweetness of your favor,
And let me sing of myself
A song of your joy.

38

Why am I stuck in the past?

The Wilcox family recently lost their home of forty years to impossible taxes. They are disoriented and anxious in their apartment. All they do is talk about "the house."

Alan was divorced by his wife after twenty-two years of marriage. He lives each day longing for the wonderful times gone by.

Laurie was downsized from a terrific job at a major high-tech firm. She sits at the coffee shop comparing her former job to all the "loser" jobs in the paper.

Gary's teenage daughter is pregnant. All he can do is look at old pictures of his little princess.

Andy retired. He tortures his wife with fond memories of his cubicle.

Barbara lost her husband to cancer. Two years later she's still setting the table for two.

Lots of folks are stuck in the past. The past has a great deal of power in our lives.

On the one hand, memories can be wonderful gifts; they can be important references for the present and an anchor for the future.

However, for some of us, remembering is not a healthy jaunt down memory lane. Instead, it becomes a way of life. For some, the past can be a prison.

So why is it that some of us are so tempted to stay behind?

One reason that occurs to me is that there are NO surprises in memories. By definition, they are things already known. That's why Andy lives inside his memories; he'd rather keep life safe and easy.

And so the past really can feel safe…and *we can control it* more easily than the present.

Something else comes to mind: the past offers us a place to hide. Laurie is afraid of a new job, so she'd rather relive the old one. The Wilcoxes felt more secure in the family home, so they try to stay there through remembering.

The past seems to protect us from the present and the future.

The past also gives us something else: a chance to change what once was. Alan spends his days reconfiguring the past in all sorts of ways that make him feel better about the present.

The past can become *a place of relief.*

Finally, I think some of us may feel guilty for moving beyond the past. I know those who have lost spouses or children. They often feel as if they are betraying their love by moving on. Barbara thinks she'll be abandoning her deceased husband if she gets on with her life—so she stays in the past with him.

For some, *the past can be a place of obligation.*

These reasons and so many more are surely understandable. The problem is, being *stuck* in the past is *not* a harmless state of mind. The past can become like a false god that isolates us, turns us inward, and leaves us unsatisfied and fearful.

The past can deny us the wholeness of our lives. Being stuck in the past steals our hope for the future.

But we don't need to stay stuck. If we need to remember something, why don't we remember Jesus?

Jesus is our Shepherd. Shepherds protect their sheep—like Laurie and the Wilcoxes; shepherds provide relief for those like Alan.

And for all those among us suffering like Barbara, there's good news: we have more than permission to leave the past behind—we have an invitation from the apostle Paul to do just that: "One thing I do: *forgetting what lies behind* and reaching forward to what lies ahead, I press on toward the goal for the prize of the upward call of God in Christ Jesus" (Philippians 3:13–14).

Food for Thought

Do I know someone who's stuck in the past?
Am I stuck in the past?
How do memories make me feel?
How can I tell if remembering is becoming harmful?
How can I use the past in healthy ways?

A PRAYER

I shall remember the deeds of
the LORD;
Surely I will remember Your
wonders of old.
I will meditate on all Your work
And muse on Your deeds.
Your way, O God, is holy;
What god is great like our God?

PSALM 77:11–13

39

Why do I always feel exhausted?

Melinda seemed typical of many young housewives in my town. She was a committed soccer mom and good wife. She did all she could for her friends and her church.

Whenever I saw Melinda, however, I noticed how tired she looked. But it wasn't the sort of harried fatigue that you find in any checkout line. Hers was that deep weariness. It was emotional exhaustion.

On a March evening several years ago, Melinda put a casserole in the oven and put the timer on. She set the table for everyone but herself. Then she went upstairs and shot herself.

Emotional exhaustion is nothing to be ignored. I'm not talking about your typical Friday-night burnout or the occasional collapse into a cushy chair. I'm talking about the kind of haunting, debilitating soul fatigue that characterizes so many lives.

For some of us, no matter how much rest we get or how many

vacations we take or even how much encouragement comes our way, we still feel utterly, totally worn out.

We need to pay attention. Exhaustion is part of our body's alarm system. Like allergies, headaches, chest pains, and nausea, exhaustion is a warning that something's wrong.

So what's wrong?

Deep exhaustion can be physical, of course. All sorts of diseases and conditions can overwhelm us. But sometimes emotional exhaustion is a symptom of outlook, a view of life that prompts endless effort.

If the doctor says we're physically healthy, we just might want to take a good look at the way we see life…our outlook. There we might find any or all these three forces at work:

Fear

Many of us fear sickness, relational struggles, economic struggles, others' power in our lives, and even disappointment. Some of us are afraid of disappointing others or embarrassing ourselves. Some of us are scared to death of God.

So what do we end up doing with the things we fear? We *work hard* at avoiding, appeasing, outmaneuvering, and overcoming them.

It's exhausting.

Shame

Some of our worlds demand excellence—excellence as parents, workers, money managers, friends, siblings… Worst of all, we feel pressure to be excellent Christians—superior examples of all we feel Scripture demands us to be.

When we fail at any of it, we feel self-contempt, shame.

So we *work hard* at doing everything just right.

It's exhausting.

Ambition

Our world abounds in tempting opportunities: money, prestige, power. The desire for these things becomes a powerful force within us. Some of us become consumed with ambition, and we race toward the Kingdom of More at full speed ahead.

It's exhausting.

Now Jesus made it pretty clear: "Come to Me, all who are weary and heavy-laden, and *I will give you rest*" (Matthew 11:28). He wants us to cast our burdens on him, to throw off the world's heavy yokes and put on *his* feather-light yoke.

But instead, exhaustion characterizes many of our lives…and that says a lot.

Exhaustion is a helpful warning that something other than Jesus is Lord of our lives.

If that something other is *fear,* we need to ask him to show us his love, for love will cast our fears away (see 1 John 4:18).

If that something is *shame,* we need to ask him to remind us of grace, which is the gift of unconditional acceptance regardless of our shortcomings (see Romans 3:23).

If it's *ambition,* we need to confess the many idols that have enslaved us (see 1 John 1:9). (If they're hard to find, imagine your life's worst-case scenario.)

If we understand *exhaustion as an alarm bell,* we can be thankful for it! Warned, we can ask the Spirit to help us see into our hearts. In so doing, we can hand over our fear, our shame, and our ambition to Jesus…and let him give us his rest.

Food for Thought

Does exhaustion characterize my life?
How would life be different if I felt rested?
Does fear, shame, or ambition drive my life?
What other things might be wearing me out?
What could resting in Jesus actually look like?

A PRAYER

*"Come unto me ye weary," dear Lord, we
    hear Thee say.
So we, heavy laden come unto Thee and pray;
Blot out the sinful past, and cleanse us from
    all dross,
Give strength for every burden, for each duty
    and each cross.*

"DAY BY DAY," AUTHOR UNKNOWN (1916)

40

Why have I stopped dreaming?

I was traveling with my older son through Tennessee, and we stopped in a small town for lunch. It was a typical, old-brick southern town, complete with a monument to the Confederacy and a lazy river by some railroad tracks. The folks were friendly enough, but there was something about the place…

Maybe it was the feet up on porch railings, the rusty cars in front yards—perhaps a few too many crumpled beer cans lying at the curb. Whatever it was, you could feel it.

As we drove away, my son looked over his shoulder as the last lifeless smokestack vanished around a curve. "They've given up," he said.

"What?"

"They've stopped hoping… They don't have any dreams left."

There have been times in my life when I've stopped dreaming. I've abandoned possibilities. I've faced my feet and shrugged.

Those are the times when life is dark.

But I well remember the expectant faces of my sons when they were little boys. I remember the lively spark of imagination that kept their young eyes wide and little hands reaching far beyond their grasp. That's when light seemed to surround them; that's when possibilities were unbounded.

Can you remember when you were a child, perhaps lying in warm grass to find faces in the clouds? That was when you dared to believe in what you could only imagine; that's when your dreams were SPECTACULAR.

Jesus said, "Whoever then humbles himself as this child, he is the greatest in the kingdom of heaven" (Matthew 18:4). I wonder if, in part, Jesus isn't urging us to return to the awed wonder of childhood. I wonder if he yearns for us to look at the clouds and see faces.

Oh, that we could be children again.

Why don't our eyes shine with hope? Why is it that so many of us dream tiny dreams—if we dream at all?

I suppose we could point to the hard realities of this life. We all know what they are. So, like that Tennessee town, we resign ourselves to what *is* and we no longer imagine what *could be*. We've unwittingly concluded that what we experience in the here and now is all there is.

How sad for us.

God never wanted us to stop dreaming. He points us always to new horizons—always to what's coming: "Forgetting what lies behind and reaching forward to what lies ahead.... For our citizenship is in heaven, from which also we eagerly wait for a Savior, the Lord Jesus Christ" (Philippians 3:13, 20).

But so few of us see ahead. So many of us face our feet and shrug.

I'm afraid we've stopped dreaming because we've lost sight of heaven. But what if we put our lives on pause from time to time and *imagined heaven*? "Eye has not seen and ear has not heard…all that God has prepared for those who love him" (1 Corinthians 2:9). Wow! Have you ever set your mind free to think about the kind of party God's got planned?

Could it mean a reunion with all those we miss so badly?

Could it mean that we will fly?

Will we see other worlds? Will we move in and out of time?

Will our pets be there?

Dare we imagine seeing some folks we don't expect to see!

But that's not all. The heavenly kingdom has already begun in the here and now. So while we're at it, maybe we could begin to imagine what *that* could mean.

How *un*conditional could unconditional love look…now?

How much more could we expect from the Spirit…now?

How great can grace really feel…now?

Dare we imagine what we're free to imagine…now?

When we begin to freshly envision the kingdom of heaven, we just may begin to dream again. And as we do, why don't we dare to imagine the most, the best, the biggest—the SPECTACULAR!

For our Lord Jesus Christ is spectacular indeed.

Food for Thought

Do I still dream of hope and possibilities? Why or why not?
Have I thought about heaven? Does it leave me empty or
   in wonder?
How grand might the kingdom be?
Have I ever stretched the possibilities?

A PRAYER

O sweet and blessed country,
The home of God's elect!
O sweet and blessed country,
That eager hearts expect!
Jesus, in mercy bring us
To that dear land of rest;
Who art, with God the Father,
And Spirit, ever blest.

SAINT BERNARD OF CLUNY
(ABT. 1100–1160) FROM
"JERUSALEM THE GOLDEN"

For every time you've tried too hard,
   fallen too far,
      or struggled too much,

the refreshing cups in this book are reminders of God's infinite grace and mercy and will renew you like cool, clear water after a long, dry walk on a dusty, uphill road.

Get a new hold on grace as you replace dashed hopes, broken dreams, and paralyzing fear with peace, joy, and purpose. Each devotional is like a cool cup of relief, comfort, revival, and sustenance.

Water is *life*. And *101 Cups of Water* will quench your thirst.

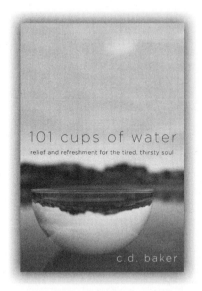